The
Changing Face of
Innovation:
Is it Shifting to Asia?

The
Changing Face of
Innovation:
Is it Shifting to Asia?

Seeram Ramakrishna
National University of Singapore, Singapore

Daniel Joo-Then Ng
Independent Strategic Advisor and Business Consultant, Singapore

World Scientific

NEW JERSEY · LONDON · SINGAPORE · BEIJING · SHANGHAI · HONG KONG · TAIPEI · CHENNAI

Published by

World Scientific Publishing Co. Pte. Ltd.

5 Toh Tuck Link, Singapore 596224

USA office: 27 Warren Street, Suite 401-402, Hackensack, NJ 07601

UK office: 57 Shelton Street, Covent Garden, London WC2H 9HE

British Library Cataloguing-in-Publication Data
A catalogue record for this book is available from the British Library.

THE CHANGING FACE OF INNOVATION
Is it Shifting to Asia?

ISBN-13 978-981-4291-58-3 (pbk)
ISBN-10 981-4291-58-7 (pbk)

In-house Editor: Sandhya Venkatesh

Typeset Stallion Press
Email: enquiries@stallionpress.com

Printed in Singapore.

FOREWORD

I grew up in the United States in the years following the Second World War, when a "Made in Japan" label on a product was synonymous with "cheap", "flimsy", and "easily broken". Products made in China, Korea, Singapore, or other Asian countries were — at least in my childhood and youthful experience — somewhere between scarce and non-existent. "Quality" was not a word that immediately sprang to mind in connection with Asian products. Neither was "innovation". The general impression of these products among Americans (at least Americans of my generation) in those early postwar days was that they were inexpensive knock-offs of American goods made with inferior materials and workmanship.

It is hardly necessary to point out today how much things have changed. Asia has become a powerhouse in science and innovation. Led by China and India, Asian nations are not just producing superb, innovative products, they are conducting frontier research and producing far more engineers and highly trained technical workers than the United States or Europe. The GDPs of these nations are expanding at a record pace, and their research and development expenditures, and hence their R&D/GDP ratios, are growing even faster. And, in even greater contrast to the way things were five decades ago, Asia has developed a solid reputation for quality and innovation. Most visible to consumers worldwide are Japanese and Korean automobiles and electronics and Chinese products of all kinds. But it does not end there. Asian nations are leading the way in creating the technologies that promise to define the 21st century, including renewable — especially solar — energy generation.

These developments are not accidental. They are the result of strategic decisions made by the governments of these nations to invest in R&D and to create networks of science and technology institutions emulating and improving on the best features of the American system — entrepreneurial research universities linked to high-tech industrial firms and well-supported government research laboratories and agencies. For a notable example of the physical and institutional expression of this strategy, one needs look no farther than Singapore's "opolis" twins, its well-known Biopolis and its more recently established Fusionopolis.

This most interesting and highly original book by Professor Seeram Ramakrishna and Daniel Joo-Then Ng of the National University of Singapore presents a vivid picture of the rise of Asian science and technology. With a wealth of statistics, charts, graphs, and illustrations, these insiders on the Asian innovation scene make a strong case for their thesis that, as the book's title states, the face of global innovation is changing and that it is indeed moving in the direction of Asia.

This is an optimistic book. Implicit in its discussion of Asia, a huge continent comprising many nations, and the authors' many comparisons of Asia versus the United States is the assumption that ancient and modern rivalries and modern geopolitical factors and conflicts internal to Asia will decline in importance relative to the shared goals of technology-based economic growth. Similarly, there is the expectation, or at least the hope, that the new face of innovation will allow the Asian nations to overcome the vast areas of poverty and backwardness that dominate large parts of their rural landscapes. In fact, the authors suggest that the innovation motivated by the need to overcome these problems will strengthen their hand in global commerce. These are laudable hopes, but they are hopes and their realization is far from certain.

As a lifelong technological optimist myself, I share the authors' upbeat view of the future. At the same time, I am compelled to ask from the perspective of an American what the shifts they describe might mean for the United States and other western nations. I can see at least two complementary implications. One is the recognition by United States policymakers of increased global competition. This has already had an impact. Impelled by the widely-read 2007 report of the United States National Academies, *Rising Above the Gathering Storm: Energizing and Employing America for a Brighter Economic Future* (conceived in response to the perception of growing competition from Asia), United States policymakers came together in a rare display of bipartisan support to pass the "America COMPETES Act", which authorizes substantial increases in federal government funding for competitiveness-related R&D as well as major investments in science, technology, engineering, and mathematics education. Although Congress did not fund these programs initially, they have begun to take off with money from the Obama Administration's 2009 stimulus program.

The second implication is that of mutual benefit arising from the worldwide expansion of scientific and technological knowledge. Despite the ill-considered efforts of some governments, science does not stop at national borders or continental margins. This is especially true with 21st-century communication and transportation technologies. As scientific capabilities in China, India, and other Asian nations have been growing, new opportunities for cooperation have also been on the rise. Asians (like other non-United States citizens) who come to the United States to study or do research often continue working with colleagues or former mentors in the United States long after they return to their native countries. The results can be seen in the rapidly increasing proportion of scientific publications with international co-authorship appearing in the pages of *Science*,

Nature, and other prestigious scientific journals. The whole in these cases and in international scientific collaboration overall is, as experience has shown, greater than the sums of individual parts.

Ramakrishna and Ng end this volume with a provocative and idealistic proposal: they call for the establishment of a Global Research Foundation to support collaborative research on pressing global problems. The value of such a body should be obvious to anyone who has given even a modest thought to the multiple crises that face humankind and the role of science and technology in their resolution. The political difficulties that would confront those with the courage to try and implement the idea, however, should be just as obvious. It would be convincing evidence that the face of innovation has truly changed if the initiative for such an enterprise were to be taken by Asian nations.

Albert H. Teich
American Association for the
Advancement of Science
Washington, DC

PROLOGUE

Two decades ago, one would hardly see books on Asia displayed in airport bookstores around the world. Fast forward ten years and it is a changed scenario! It is now uncommon to find a bookstore that does not carry books, magazines or newspapers that are related to Asia. Nowadays, it is common that social media and conversations among people often make comparisons of USA and Europe to Asia. The resurgence of Asia after several centuries of slumber in the economic, social, cultural, and political arena is a subject of frequent and intense discussion among business leaders, thinkers, academics, politicians, policy makers, opinion leaders, journalists, and social media. According to an article in Newsweek dated 8 September 2008, 90 percent of the world's engineers will be in Asia by 2011. The same report says that China and India will by the same year be producing five times the number of engineers that USA is producing.

Going by Global Domestic Product, GDP, Asia is home to the second (China) and third (Japan) largest economies of the world. Going by purchasing power parity (PPP) GDP, Asia is home to the second (China), third (Japan) and fourth (India) largest economies of the world.

For several decades, USA has been the major funder of research and innovation in the world, followed by the European Union.

2006 was a watershed year for the modern world. Global research and development expenditure, for the first time in human history, exceeded US$ 1 trillion. At the same time, the growth rate of research and development expenditure of Asia as a whole surpassed that of USA and Europe in 2009, signifying the building up of momentum of spending in the building up of more research and development bases in Asia. This marks the beginning of a sea of change in the relative contribution of Asia Pacific and Atlantic nations in the increased setting up of more research centres by governments and multi-national enterprises in Asia Pacific, scientific publications and patents.

Global research and development spending continued to increase as indicated in Figure P. 1. The financial crisis of 2008 did not dampen the growth for 2009. Notably, a bigger portion of the increases is coming from Asia (See Table P.1).

As seen from Table P.1, in 2009 Asia topped annual R&D spending for the first time ever since the tracking of global R&D spending began. Of the US$ 386.9 billion, 80 percent come from Japan, China and India. China had the highest growth: China's R&D spending grew by 16.1 percent: from US$ 122.7 billion in 2008 to US$ 142.4 billion in 2009.

Global Research and Development Spending
GERD PPP*
Billions of US Dollars

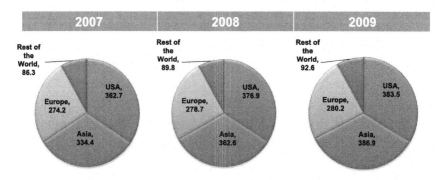

Figure P.1:   Global R&D Spending Continues to Rise in 2009.

Source: Battelle, Columbus, Ohio, and R&D Magazine, December 2008.

Note: *PPP: Purchasing Power Parity; GERD: Gross Domestic Expenditure on R&D.

Table P.1: Asia tops the share of R&D spending in 2009.

2009 Estimates of Global Spending of Research and Innovation Dollars
Share of Total R&D Spending

	Asia	USA	Europe
Research & Development Funding in 2009	US$ 386.9 billion	US$ 383.5 billion	US$ 280.2 billion
% of Global Spending	33.8%	33.6%	24.5%

Source: Battelle, Columbus, Ohio, and R&D Magazine, Dec 2008.

Leading independent think-tanks and prestigious national academies of several nations in Europe and USA foresee a corresponding rise in Asia's leadership in the fields of research and innovation. They suggest that policy makers, the research community, the public and the younger generation be prepared for the competition and the changing dynamics of the human world.

For the past two hundred years, nations surrounding the Atlantic Ocean led research and innovation for the modern world. In recent years, Asian nations surrounding the Pacific Ocean have increasingly joined their ranks. This encourages us to ask the following questions:

Does this mean a renaissance in Asian innovation?

If so, does this resurgence signal a long-term shift of the centre of gravity of research and innovation from the Atlantic to Pacific, or is it just a passing cloud?

Does Asia possess the cultural history and current potential for scholarship and innovation?

In this book, we try to highlight key enablers, the forces of innovation, influencers and spoilers of this emerging trend. We also suggest some strategies that nations can adopt to leverage research and innovation.

With the global mobility of talent, we see that technological leadership is spreading globally. Many trans-national companies are moving their research and development (R&D) centres into Asia Pacific, and this shift is gaining momentum. China and India's domestic market potential and opportunities are having a reverse brain drain effect. The "intellectual diaspora" of China and India are either returning to their "homeland" or cooperating closely with their counterparts in R&D or business enterprises. Many Asian governments are providing incentives in the form of special tax concessions or infrastructures for test-bedding of ideas.

Policy makers in Asia are making huge contributions towards transforming universities to become inter-disciplinary and international research intensive institutions. Women and talented young people are being encouraged to engage themselves in R&D so as to produce better solutions to societal challenges of global nature.

In the first millennium, Asia was the centre of gravity of innovation. This gradually shifted to Europe and then to North America in the second half of the second millennium. The face of innovation is changing. The beginning of the third millennium is witnessing a shifting of the center of innovation back to Asia. Thomas L. Friedman (*New York Times*)[1] saw the world becoming flat. We see innovation going full circle. The same factors which made our world flat are also causing innovation to go full circle.

Here, we identify 13 reasons that support the likelihood of a shift of center of gravity of research and innovation to Asia. We will elaborate on these in subsequent chapters:

1. About 60 percent of the world's population resides in Asia, meaning one in every two humans is Asian. According to forecasts, the proportion of Asians in the world will remain unchanged despite the growth of the current

---

[1] Friedman T.L., *The World is Flat*, 2005.

world population from 6.8 billion to 8.9 billion in 2050. Currently 11 percent and 5 percent of the world population live in Europe and North America, respectively. According to the forecast, in year 2050, Europe and North America will have 7 percent and 4.4 percent of the world's population.

2. Asia is home to major ancient civilizations of the world that contributed to the earlier inventions of humankind. In the current age, we see a repetition of that trend — human necessities, fueled by societal challenges and supported by growing economic wealth, are creating both capacity and capabilities for innovation.

3. Asia is home to the majority of the world's youth, who are ambitious, motivated and working hard to achieve their dreams. The combined force of their efforts will likely lead them to shape, in far-reaching and meaningful ways, the future of our world in the 21st century.

4. Asia's share of global GDP is nearly 50 percent, indicating a growing economic capacity to shape the future. Dramatic economic growth is being witnessed in countries like Singapore. In just over 50 years, the Singapore economy has grown 125 times, from S$2 billion to S$250 billion.

5. Asia's share of high-technology manufacturing of the world is 50 percent, while one-quarter of total manufacturing of the world is high-technology manufacturing.

6. Most of the recent growth in the workforce for global total research and innovation is happening in Asia. According to one estimate, the global total research work-force is close to about ten million — the highest ever in the history of mankind, meaning a large number of Asians are involved in the innovation process.

7. Asians are known for having high affinity towards modern technology-enabled products. The younger generation are especially proud to own high-technology goods with wide ranges of features.

8. In recent years, large numbers of Asians have been trav-elling widely to all corners of the world and in the process

becoming directly conversant with best practices prevailing in the world. In addition, the wide reach of modern social media which includes the internet, television and radio programmes delivered in their mother tongues within their homes has enabled vast populations of Asia to learn more about and appreciate other advanced societies. This has awakened many Asians, and the mystery in their minds concerning the rest of the world is disappearing. The exposure has also enabled Asians to discuss societal issues far more openly, confidently and constructively. There is a growing appetite for new knowledge and social advancement across Asia. These developments are transforming the minds of many Asians. They now believe that they are free to invent themselves, and destiny is believed to be human-made instead of being assumed to be predetermined. There is a shift from non-material aspirations to material aspirations.

9. Assisted by recent rapid economic growth and necessities imposed by national challenges, Asian nations are becoming test beds for the experimentation of new innovations. This creates a virtuous cycle of implementation of innovative solutions, and resources to support research and innovation, and thereby develop new innovations. For example, many greenfield development projects in Asia are adopting higher energy-efficient and environmentally-friendly standards in the construction of new buildings and cities, power generation plants, and manufacturing plants. Given the economic and market sizes of these nations, they are likely to set new benchmarks that will increasingly influence the success of future innovations.

10. Similar to the way America benefited from the migration of brilliant scientists and innovators from Europe in the 20th century, Asia is poised to reap benefits from returning talented scientists, engineers and policy makers who are educated and trained at the best universities in Europe and USA of the 21st century. These talented people are

maintaining strong ties with their alma maters and their networks in Europe and USA. This unique situation provides a new paradigm: Asia and the rest of the world are well-placed to partner in research and implementation of innovative solutions to the benefit of everyone.

11. In addition to enhanced research investments and an increasingly younger generation, other key enablers of innovation are falling into place in Asia. Asia is expanding the institutes of higher learning sector by opening more universities, with the goal of improving the university enrolment rate of high school graduates from 20 percent to 30 percent. In addition, Asian countries are also boosting the number of students trained in technical skills and vocational training.

12. Thanks to the proponents of full disclosure of findings of basic research, scientists around the world are able to access the latest breakthroughs as soon as they are published in literature. Access to peer-reviewed journals via the internet has broadened the worldwide access to scientific advancements at an unprecedented speed — a dramatic change when we remember that not too long ago researchers had to wait for months to get a copy of published journal papers. In contrast, today, research communities around the world are far more well-connected and integrated than ever before. We consider this openness and broader access to knowledge to be an important enabler of Asia's strong participation in research and innovation endeavours.

13. Big multi-national enterprises are acting according to their strategic analysis and insights of the changing world, and meeting the expectations of diverse national and international investors. They are at the forefront of market expansion beyond their native countries. There are many multi-national enterprises with major involvement in markets in Asia. They have understood the changing face of innovation much before the policy makers did, and are

practicing open innovation by leveraging on research and innovations occurring in different parts of the world and augmenting their own in-house innovation and development. In the process, they are accelerating innovation and reducing the major components of its costs. We consider the open sourcing of innovation and integrative practices of trans-world companies as yet another key enabler of Asia's increased participation in the global research and innovation value chain.

There are always two sides to a coin. While the factors above provide an upbeat scenario for a strong representation of Asia in research and innovation, one cannot underestimate the challenges ahead. Many Asian nations, though growing increasingly richer economically, face a widening income gap between the rich and poor. This feeling of inequality may affect the confidence of tax payers when it comes to endorsing research and open innovation practices.

Thanks to the progress of growing collaboration between countries over the years, researchers from different nations are increasingly able to travel beyond borders and meet other researchers in their respective fields and make long-lasting connections, exchange ideas and establish win–win research partnerships. However, we feel that the forms of international cooperation that currently exist are sub-optimal due to limitations that arise due to conditions posed by funding agencies and excessive expectations and management of intellectual property. With increasing competition for growth and jobs, the temptation for protectionism and conflicts are real. While competition is necessary for research excellence and creative innovation, pure competition without appropriate cooperation leads to the duplication of efforts and less efficient use of valuable resources. Strenuous, visionary long-term efforts are needed to avert this downward trend. The current lack of a global research fund towards pre-competitive research to discover novel solutions for global societal challenges does not help to improve the situation.

The challenge ahead is how to converge towards an integrated global innovation community that is positioned to develop novel ideas and solutions to address global challenges for the well-being and progress of humanity. This is an opportune time to consider the paradigm shift towards a Global Research Foundation (GRF), to find solutions for global societal challenges such as rapid population growth, sustainable economical growth, rapid urbanisation, effective leveraging of information and communication technologies, water scarcity, sustainable energy, climate change, ageing issues, emerging and infectious diseases, safety, security and quality of food supplies.

ACKNOWLEDGEMENTS

References and footnotes provide partial acknowledgements of our indebtedness to all the earlier thinkers and writers. Without the advent of the internet and search engines like Google plus statistical information from institutions and organisations, we would not have managed to complete this book. Many thanks and gratitude to all relatives, friends and colleagues who read and critiqued the draft manuscript. Special thanks to Albert Teich who so graciously agreed to write the Foreword of the this book.

LIST OF ABBREVIATIONS

Total Primary Energy Supply (TPES)	Total Primary Energy Supply (TPES) is made up of production + imports - exports - international aviation bunkers +/− stock changes. For the world total, international marine bunkers and international aviation bunkers are not substracted from the TPES.
ICT	Information and Communication Technology
S&T	Science and Technology
WHO	World Health Organisation
OECD	Organisation of Economic Co-operation and Development
GRF	Global Research Foundation
IHL	Institution of Higher Learning
ROW	Rest of World

General conversion factors for energy

To: From:	TJ	Gcal	Mtoe	MBtu	GWh
	multiply by:				
TJ	1	238.8	2.388×10^{-5}	947.8	0.2778
Gcal	4.1868×10^{-3}	1	10^{-7}	3.968	1.163×10^{-3}
Mtoe	4.1868×10^{4}	10^{7}	1	3.968×10^{7}	11630
MBtu	1.0551×10^{-3}	0.252	2.52×10^{-8}	1	2.931×10^{-4}
GWh	3.6	860	8.6×10^{-5}	3412	1

ABOUT THE AUTHORS

Professor Seeram Ramakrishna, FREng, FNAE, FAAAS is an advisor and a sought-after speaker worldwide on global trends of higher education, scientific research, and innovation. He participates in round table discussions organized by various think tanks, World Bank, OECD, and ASEAN. He was trained as a materials engineer at the University of Cambridge, and received general management training from the Harvard University. Thomson Reuters ISI Web of Knowledge places him among the top one percent of materials scientists worldwide (ESI rank is 30). He is an elected international fellow of major engineering societies in Singapore, ASEAN, India, UK and USA. He is a professor at the National University of Singapore, and held several senior leadership positions which include Dean of Engineering, Vice-President of research strategy, Vice-President of International Federation of Engineering Education Societies, and Founding Chair of Global Engineering Deans Council. His passion led to global scientific research and innovation partnerships among world-class institutions around the world in healthcare, energy, water and sustainability.

Daniel Joo-Then Ng, is an independent Strategic Advisor and Business Consultant who nurtures/develops people and provides strategic advice to institutions and non-profit organizations. His educational qualifications are in Applied

Chemistry (BSc (Hons), University of Singapore) and General Management (Singapore Institute of Management and Dartmouth College, New Hampshire, USA), he has worked more than 30 years in Singapore, UK, Indonesia and China, overseeing regional operations of multinational companies involved in Water, Energy, Environment; Food Quality & Safety Solutions and In-vitro Medical Devices. He has performed different roles: from manufacturing and supply chain management, sales and marketing, general management, country management to regional corporate and strategic management. His passion is in pioneering operations and developing the unique potential of individuals and organization. Companies he worked for included subsidiaries and affiliates of Nalco Chemical Company, Silliker Group Corporation and bioMerieux. Institutions he worked for included National University of Singapore, and he is associated with Nanyang Polytechnic, Singapore and Jiangnan University, Wuxi, Jiangsu Province, China.

DISCLAIMER

The views expressed in this book are those of the authors and do not reflect the official policy or position of the National University of Singapore.

"Human ideate, invent, innovate to progress, prosper and sustain" — Seeram Ramakrishna and Daniel Ng

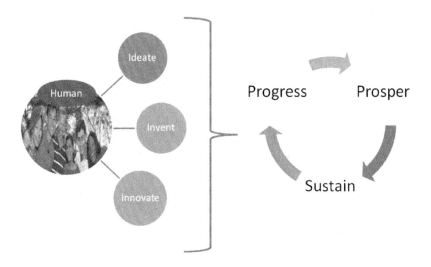

CONTENTS

Chapter 1

ASIA'S SPIRIT OF INNOVATION

Asia is home to major ancient civilisations, which include, in today's terminology, China and India. Their early inventions, spanning several hundreds of years, are forerunners of the advancements and lifestyles we are accustomed to today. With the support of advanced analytical tools and techniques, scientists, archeologist and historians continue to uncover the origin of these ancient inventions.[2]

During his travels to China in the 13th century, Marco Polo (from Europe) encountered Chinese civilisations which were more technologically advanced than Europe. Arab scholars were also more advanced than the Europeans in the same era. This confirms that Asia used to be the centre of innovation in the first millennium. This gradually shifted to Europe and then to North America in the latter half of the second millennium. Now, the beginning of the third millennium is witnessing the return of the center of innovation to Asia.

What is "Asia"? How different or similar is it to European Union (EU) or the USA?

---

[2] What is the relationship between creativity, invention and innovation? These words are used interchangeably, but they are different. Creativity is a new idea, a flash of inspiration that identifies a new pattern. It could have existed, yet undiscovered. Invention is making a prototype of the idea to show others and test to see if it works. Finally, an innovation is an invention that changes old patterns and has been put to use by the customers. — *The Book of Invention* by Ian Harrison.

Asia is a geographical region of the world that comprises many countries including:

Afghanistan, Cambodia, China, India, Indonesia, Japan, Laos, Malaysia, Myanmar, North Korea, the Philippines, Pakistan, Singapore, South Korea, Thailand and Vietnam.

Many of these countries came into being after World War II. During this time their current national borders were formed. Even though these nations are collectively referred to as "Asia", they are not held together by the same degree of common purpose as the European Union and the nations of Iberian–America.

Asia is an artificial phrase that has become vogue over time. It is a highly heterogeneous region with rich and poor nations, resource-endowed and resource-poor nations, highly democratic and less democratic nations, single language and multilingual nations, nations with single and multiple ethnic groups, small nations and big nations in terms of population and land mass, technologically well-advanced and less-advanced nations, and peaceful nations and nations constantly embroiled in internal and external conflicts. Furthermore, the diets, customs, culture and belief systems vary considerably as one traverses Asia.

The heterogeneity of Asia is perplexing and, at the same time, incredibly interesting. People have begun to recognise Asia as a distinct geographical region of the world with shared challenges, whose influence on the future of the rest of the world cannot be ignored.

Let us do a quick survey of key ancient inventions and continual innovations by Asian countries/civilisations that had a great impact on the development of science and technology and progress of humanity.

The four great inventions of ancient China were the compass (see Figure 1.1), gunpowder, papermaking and printing.

Figure 1.1:   Chinese compass (circa fourth century B.C.).

COMPASS

The earliest compasses were reported to exist in China around fourth century B.C. Compasses were made of lodestone, a type of magnetite (magnetic iron ore). The Chinese discovered that an elongated lodestone freely suspended or free to rotate would tend to set its long axis to a north–south direction. The handle of the spoon points to the south. They also discovered that this characteristic could be transferred to an iron/steel needle or object by stroking it with a lodestone, for example in the form of a fish-shaped iron leaf (see Figure 1.2).

The compass enabled mariners to determine the direction of travel even when the weather was foggy and the sky was overcast. This enabled mariners to navigate safely, away from the coast line and head into the open seas. The discovery of the compass laid the foundation for a navigation system for exploration and sea trade leading to the Age of Exploration.[3] Chinese Admiral Zheng He was the first person to officially use the

---

[3] Age of Exploration — the period in history starting from the 15th century to 17th century, during which Europeans mariners explored and mapped the world.

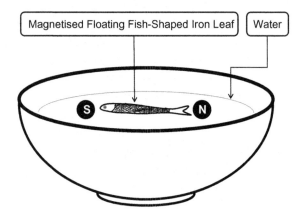

Figure 1.2:   The floating fish-shaped iron leaf compass.[4]

compass for navigation during the eight sea voyages between 1405 and 1433.

GUNPOWDER

The Chinese invention of gun powder is mixture of potassium nitrate or saltpeter, charcoal and sulphur. When ignited, this mixture produces a huge volume of gas (about 274 to 360 cubic centimeters of gas per gram of powder) and temperatures that range from 2,100 degree celsius to 2,700 degree celsius. Gunpowder was invented during the ninth century by Chinese alchemists.

The invention of gunpowder revolutionised warfare and transformed the power balances of the world. Modern fireworks that we enjoy watching are made of gunpowder and metal powders.

Today, the innovation of gunpowder in China has gone into the development of modern fireworks that are used in celebration of major events around the world. The literal

---

[4] The floating fish-shaped iron leaf compass was described in the Wujing Zongyao "Collection of the Most Important Military Techniques"; a Chinese military compendium written in 1044 AD under the Imperial Order.

translation of the Chinese words for fireworks is "fire flower". The latest spectacular fireworks display held during the opening and closing of the Beijing Olympics in 2008 is a demonstration of how far the innovations of gunpowder with metal oxides has gone to enhance the celebratory impact of major celebrations and events around the world.

PAPER MAKING AND PRINTING

China was the first nation to invent paper. Around 50 A.D., eunuch Tsai Lun from the eastern Han dynasty invented the prototype of modern paper with a mixture of wood fibers from the bark of mulberry trees, bamboo fibres and water, and pressed this mixture onto a textile cloth on a bamboo frame. The pores in the textile cloth allowed the moisture to drain out forming a layer of paper.

Ancient China's long history of hand carving and invention of paper led to the invention of wood block printing. The Chinese text is first written on a thin piece of paper. This paper is glued face down onto a wooden plate. A carver will carve the "reversed" character onto this wooden plate. Ink is then applied onto this wooden plate and pressed onto paper. This was the genesis of wood-block printing in China.

For every new page, a new wood-block had to be carved. This took a great amount of skilled manpower and materials. Bi Sheng (Song Dynasty, 960–1279) invented the carving of individual characters on a small block of moistened clay. These individual blocks were hardened by fire and could be used whenever required. These individual "movable blocks" would be glued to an iron plate to print out a page. These individual clay blocks could then be detached and reconfigured for a new page of text.

The Chinese paper-making invention was easy to mass produce and the Chinese invention of wood-block printing allowed for the easy duplication of information and knowledge.

The invention of paper and printing is an epoch-making event in human history. These inventions enabled the recording, dissemination and distribution of knowledge which in turn stimulated more innovations and discoveries throughout the ages.

SEISMOGRAPH

The Indian Tectonic Plate caused frequent earthquakes in China. In 130 A.D., Zhang Heng invented the first earthquake detector using an elaborate bronze vessel inside which a pendulum hung motionless until a tremor moved it. The instrument resembled a wine jar (see Figure 1.3). It has eight Chinese

Figure 1.3: Chinese Seismograph — When an earthquake occurs, the dragon will release a ball into the mouth of the toad.

traditional dragon figurines on the body of the jar with the heads aligning to the eight principal directions of the compass. Eight toad figurines, with their mouths opened, are placed below the eight dragons. It was known that when an earthquake occurred as far as four hundred miles away, one of the dragons would release its ball into the mouth of the toad to indicate the direction of the occurrence.

SILK AND CHINESE EMBROIDERY

Silk and Chinese embroidery is a classical intertwining of innovation and art form. China's discovery of silk and development of sericulture[5] is a great historical contribution to human society. The discovery of silk production is dated back to 5,000 years ago in China. Silk and Chinese embroidery has made great contributions towards tapestries, textile and fashion in Europe. Chinese silk became much sought after by the aristocrats and nobility of Europe. In 1877, a German geographer, Ferdinand von Richthofen, named the transcontinental trade routes from China to Central Asia and Europe as the famous "Silk Road".

ENGINEERING — GRAND CANAL OF CHINA

The building of the Grand Canal of China started in 486 B.C. Till today, it remains the longest and oldest man-made canal in the world. It served as a model for transportation, flood control and water management.

Different technologies were used to construct each of the canals. They were built to serve different purposes. The scale and size of any man-made canals over the centuries could not surpass the Chinese Grand Canal (see Figure 1.4).

---

[5] Sericulture, also known as silk farming, involves the rearing of silkworms for the production of raw silk.

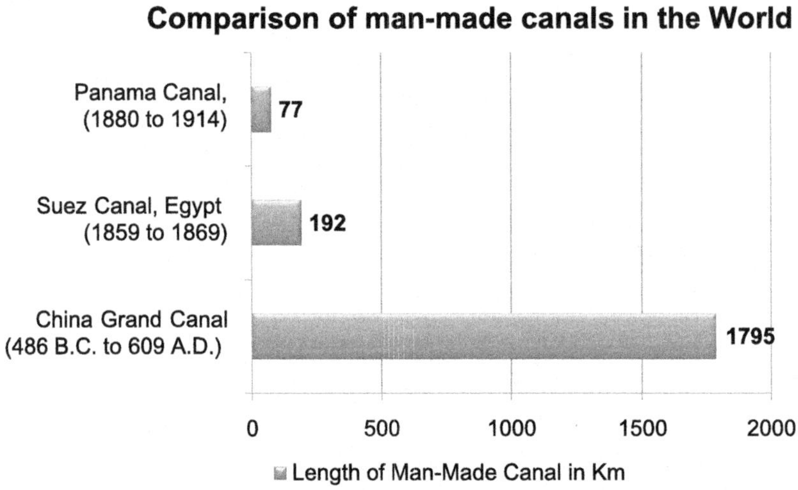

Comparison of man-made canals in the World

Figure 1.4: The China Grand Canal is about nine times longer than the Suez Canal and 23 times longer than the Panama Canal.

MATHEMATICS

Science and modern society cannot function without a numeration system for purposes such as the simple tallying of numbers. The global financial meltdown of 2008 showed the importance and great impact of finance, which requires a numeration system. It all started with simple tallies some 17,000 years ago using single strokes ('I') on surfaces such as bones. Number language was known to be practiced by several ancient civilisations. A better numeration system based on the derivative of the alphabet arose in India from 200 B.C. to 600 A.D. and replaced all other numeration systems. Arab traders picked up the new numeration system, which subsequently spread to Europe.

Ancient Indians and Babylonians were known to have followed the notion of "zero". At about 100 B.C. Pingala (India) developed a system of binary enumeration that could be converted to decimal numerals. The concepts of circles, squares, rectangles, and triangles were known to have been developed by ancient Indian scholars. Developments in geometry and algorithms led to innovations in architecture, and developments in astronomy helped to predict the weather, such as monsoonal seasons in India. Indians' deep interest in spirituality and thinking in astronomical time spans have in many ways influenced them to take special interest and focus on precise celestial calculations. In 500 A.D., celestial constants such as the earth's rotation per solar orbit, days per solar orbit, and days per lunar orbit were calculated by Aryabhata from India.

Srinivasa Ramanujan (1887–1920) developed his own theory of divergent series and worked on the Riemann series, elliptic integrals, hypergeometric series, and functional equations of the zeta function. In recognition of all these mathematical contributions, Srinivasa Ramanujan became the first Indian to be elected to the Royal Society, UK, in 1918. Many of his discoveries are applied to physics, particularly crystallography[6] and string theory. Crystallography is a tool that is often employed by material scientists. In biology, scientists use X-ray crystallography as the primary method for determining molecular conformations of biological macromolecules such as proteins and nucleic acids including DNA.

PRECIOUS METALS

India is known to have made metallurgical advancements in metal extraction and alloying processes at the same time as the other major ancient civilisations. The seven metre-high rust-free Iron Pillar of Delhi is a good example of their skills (see Figure 1.5).

---

[6] Crystallography is an experimental science of determining the arrangement of atoms in solids.

Figure 1.5: The Iron Pillar of Delhi, fourth century A.D.

Advanced skills for processing precious metals allowed Indians to accumulate a wealth of gold and silver for centuries. It is often quoted that there is more gold held privately by Indians than the gold reserves of the world's largest bank, though this has never been officially confirmed.

According to an estimate, there is around 20,000 to 25,000 tonnes (1 tonne = 1,000 kg or 32,151 troy ounce) of gold in India's households (*The Economic Times*).[7] India is currently the world's largest consumer of gold, as it imported 27 percent (769 tonnes) of the global demand in 2007 and 23 percent (660 tonnes) of the total gold demand in 2008 (World Council of Gold).[8]

---

[7] *The Economic Times*, India, 5 July 2009.
[8] World Gold Council, http://www.gold.org/.

IMMUNOLOGY

Variolation is an ancient form of vaccination that originated in China and India in 200 B.C. Smallpox was the first disease that used the variolation principle of intentionally inoculating a healthy person with fluid taken from people with mild cases of smallpox. They found that by doing so, people are protected against severe cases of smallpox.

Edward Jenner (1749–1823), an English surgeon, discovered in 1796 that by using the same variolation principle and with cowpox instead as the source to inoculate a healthy patient, he or she will be immunised to the deadly smallpox disease. Jenner called this procedure vaccination. This medical breakthrough has saved countless lives. Edward Jenner then became known as the "Father of Immunology".[9]

This interestingly showed the spirit of innovation in the early days when immunisation began in Asia. If the scholars then had similar access to the communication technology of today and the comfort of speedy air travel, how much more progress would have been achieved through collaborative research!

TERTIARY EDUCATION — THE START AND LATER REVIVAL OF AN ANCIENT UNIVERSITY IN INDIA

Between the 5th and 12th centuries, India became home to Nalanda University, one of the world's first residential universities (see Figure 1.6). Nalanda attracted thousands of scholars and students from around the world to learn philosophy, logic

---

[9] Britannica Guide to the 100 Most Influential Scientists.

Figure 1.6: Nalanda University (5 A.D.-12 A.D.).

theology, astronomy, mathematics, medicine, and Buddhist and Vedic texts. Over 10,000 students from China, Thailand, Indonesia, Japan, Korea, Persia, Tibet and Turkey came to Nalanda to be taught by over 2,000 faculty members. When Nalanda lost its grandeur at the end of the 12th century, famous European universities, such as Oxford University, and others in England, Bologna and Italy were being established. World-class universities such as Yale or Harvard were established in USA between 1701 and 1879.

At the 2006 December Asian Summit, a decision was made to revive Nalanda University.

A group of eminent personalities from around the world including Nobel Laureate Amartya Sen and former Singapore foreign minister, George Yeo will mentor this project. A fully functional Nalanda International University will revive the spirit of learning in areas such as philosophy, Buddhism and comparative religion, historical studies, languages, ecology and environment, international relations and peace and leadership and management.

SEVEN WONDERS OF THE WORLD

Throughout the history of mankind, various lists of "Wonders of the World" were compiled to recognise outstanding and spectacular structures or monuments that are engineered and built by mankind.

The following are the Seven Wonders of the Ancient World:

1. Great Pyramid of Giza, Egypt
2. Hanging Gardens of Babylon, Al Hillah, Iraq
3. Statue of Zeus at Olympia, Greece
4. Temple of Artemis at Ephesus, Turkey
5. Mausoleum of Maussollos at Halicarnassus, Turkey
6. Colossus of Rhodes, Greece
7. Lighthouse of Alexandria, Egypt

The Seven Wonders of the Medieval World include:

1. Stonehenge, Wiltshire, UK
2. Colosseum, Rome, Italy
3. Catacombs of Kom el Shoqafa, Alexandria, Egypt
4. Great Wall of China, China
5. Porcelain Tower of Nanjing, China
6. Hagia Sophia, Istanbul, Turkey
7. Leaning Tower of Pisa, Italy

The New Seven Wonders of the World

In 2007, over 100 million people from all parts of the world voted through internet, phones and text messages for the new 7 wonders of the world (see Figure 1.7).

The New Seven Wonders of the World, in alphabetic order, include:

1. Chichen Itza, Yucatan, Mexico
2. Christ the Redeemer, Rio de Janerio, Brazil
3. Colosseum, Rome, Italy
4. Great Wall of China, China
5. Machu Picchu, Cuzco, Peru.
6. Petra, Jordan
7. Taj Mahal, India

13

Figure 1.7: Official New Seven Wonders of the World voted by over 100 million people.

Out of the new Seven Wonders of the World, two are from Asia: The Great Wall of China and the Taj Mahal in India.

Great Wall of China in China (220 B.C. and 1368–1644 AD)

The Great Wall of China is the world's longest man-made structure, about 6,400 km (4,000 miles) long. It stretches from Shanhai Pass (Hebei) in the east to Lop Nur (Xinjiang) in the west. About 65 percent of the length of the Great Wall of China is equivalent to the direct distance from San Francisco to New York, which is 4,156 km (2,582 miles). Furthermore, the direct distance from Paris to Moscow, which is 2,482 km (1,542 miles), covers 39 percent of the length of the Great Wall of China.

The Great Wall of China was built as a fortification structure for defensive purposes as there were raids conducted by Mongol, Turkic and various nomadic tribes.

14

Taj Mahal of India

The Taj Mahal was a spectacular monument built by the Emperor Shah Jahan as a symbol of eternal love for his wife, Mumtaz Mahal, in 1653. The Mughal architecture combines elements from Persian, Indian and Islamic architecture styles.

The Asian spirit of innovation is driven by the desire to meet the needs of society and commemorate loved ones, or simply due to their sense of adventure. It is good to see more people expressing their interests towards Asian civilisations. In the first millennium, we saw the impact of Asian innovation on civilisation. In the second wave, we saw European Renaissance contributions towards the industrialisation of the world. In the third wave, we saw how North America, innovative culture impacted the global world. Today, we see a fourth wave happening in Asia Pacific. This shows the amazing renaissance happening in Asia in this 21st century! The Asian spirit of innovation is coming full circle.

Chapter 2

ENABLERS — FORCES
OF INNOVATION

We are living in an unprecedented time in history. For the first time, global investment in research and development exceeded US$ 1 trillion in 2006. For the first time in 2010, Asia had the highest percentage contribution in global research and development investments (see Figure 2.1). For the first time, our generation will see a rapid growth of new universities around the world, especially in developing countries. For the first time, the young minds of the 21st century will have to shoulder and support bigger proportions of silver generations. For the first time, the openness and wider access to knowledge is raising awareness from intellects around the world via the internet, mobile phones and satellite television. For the first time, the open business environment and test-bedding innovations are globally driven by mega size projects carried out by multinational participations, e.g. China adopted German technology to build the Shanghai Maglev train system.

Over the last few years, the share of R&D spending in Asia has increased. In 2010, it exceeded the USA by 1.06 percent, which is four billion US dollars according to the 2010 Global R&D Forecast (see Figure 2.2 and Table 2.1). Hence, there is a significant increase in the share of R&D spending in Asia.

Typically, two-thirds of R&D expenditure goes to manpower costs while one-third goes to the purchase of materials, equipment and infrastructure. The wage structure in Asia is

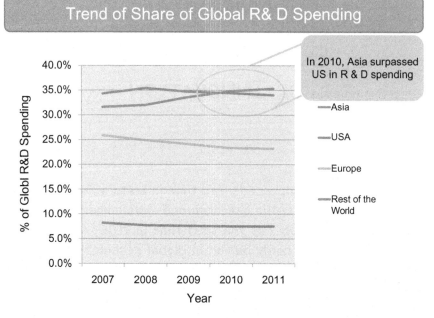

Figure 2.1: Share of R&D spending in Asia is increasing.
Source: 2009 Global R&D Forecast — sponsored by Battelle and R&D Magazine.[10]

considerably lower than that of the USA and the European Union. This means that for the same amount of expenditure, more researchers can be engaged in Asia than in the USA and European Union nations. In the short run, research volume does not always equate to research excellence and innovation. However, over a time period of a decade or two, changes in the value system, together with a growth in research volume, are likely to create significant opportunities for excellence in innovation. In the past, opportunities and tools for Asian scientists were primarily provided by USA and European countries. With the increased R&D spending in Asian nations, Asian scientists

---

[10] 2009 Global R&D Funding Forecast, Dec 2008, R&D Magazine.

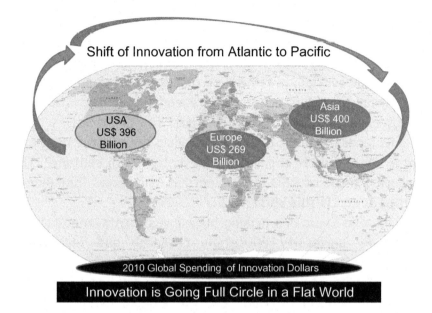

Figure 2.2: The share of R&D spending in 2009. Asia was the top spender in 2009.

Source: Battelle, R&D Magazine, 2011 Global R&D Funding Forecast

Table 2.1: Global R&D Spending and Forecast — Asia became the big spender from 2010.

Global R&D Spending and Forecast					
Year	2007	2008	2009	2010	2011
Measurement Units	GERD PPP* Billions US$	GERD PPP* Billions US$	GERD PPP* Billions US$	GERD PPP* Billions US$	GERD PPP* Billions US$
Asia	334.4	359.0	372.5	400.4	421.1
USA	362.7	397.6	383.6	395.8	405.8
Europe	274.2	278.8	267.0	268.6	276.6
Rest of the World	86.3	86.4	83.9	85.8	89.0
Global Total	1057.6	1121.8	1107.0	1150.6	1192.0
Ref: Battelle, R&D Magazine	2009 Global forecast	2010 Global forecast	2011 Global forecast	2011 Global forecast	2011 Global forecast
Edition Date	Dec 2008	Dec 2009	Dec 2010	Dec 2010	Dec 2010

Note: *PPP means Purchasing Power Parity.

are gaining increased access to advanced tools and opportunities at home. Many of these new research tools are the latest state-of-art equipment. There are several implications on the future of innovation, which will be discussed later. It indicates that Asian countries are taking research and innovation far more seriously as compared to the past few countries.

This leads us to the question: will Asia become the next epicentre of research and innovation in the 21st century? The increasing trend of R&D investments in Asia shows that Asia is pointing towards this shift.

China and India are making huge investments in education, specifically university education, research and technology. China, India, Japan, Korea, Taiwan, Singapore and most of the other Asian countries are placing a higher emphasis on education and innovation to build new and relevant local models to meet the societal needs of the growing middle class as well as the lower-income class. While the USA has the highest R&D spending in the area of military applications, Japan focuses on meeting consumers' needs. As for China, in 1995 there was an unprecedented move to engage the International Development Research Centre (IDRC) in Canada to work with the State Science and Technology Commission in China to conduct a joint review of China's experience in science and technology reform, which took place in the past decade.[11] Many different local models that focus on meeting societal needs will make their economy less dependent on exports. The successful new innovations can then be exported to the rest of the world. A good recent example is the GE R&D centre in China that bases innovations on the portable PC-based ultrasound device that was

---

[11] A Decade of Reform resulting from the Science and Technology Policy in China and the efforts by the International Development Research Centre, Canada, and State Science and Technology Commission, People's Republic of China.

originally conceived in the GE Israel R&D centre. The innovative portable PC-based ultrasound device cost only USD 15,000 per set.[12] This low-price innovation made it affordable for the China health care system and village clinics. In India, the GE R&D centre developed a hand-held electrocardiogram that cost about US$ 1,000 per set and which can be afforded by village doctors. All the equipment is now being exported to the USA for use by emergency and crisis service centres. We can be certain that many new low-cost but equally effective in its utilitarian benefits will catch on to be used in different ways in all developed countries. A similar hospital-based equipment in USA costs many times more than these new innovations.

Asia is positioned to generate more new products and services that are important to society. China and India are constantly searching for modern technologies that can help them to make advancements. Japan, South Korea, Taiwan, and Singapore have already shifted their focus from production and manufacturing-based industries to knowledge-intensive industries. With a greater momentum in innovation, Asia could become the next centre for innovation, research and development in the 21st century.

Though the political will of Asia Pacific countries to innovate to move towards a knowledge-intensive economy is strong, there are many obstacles that leaders would face. One key societal challenge is to lift about 1.8 billion people in Asia Pacific out of poverty (people who live on less than US$ 2 a day).

The leaders in Asia Pacific countries will have to harness relevant innovations that can convert adversity into advantages. There are many ways to use innovation to overcome these adversities.

---

[12] Jeffrey R Immelt, Vijay Govindarajan, and Chris Timble, How GE is Disrupting Itself, *Harvard Business Review*, October 2009.

First, innovations can be adapted from existing technologies. For example, instead of having traditional land-lines for telecommunications, solar-generated electricity can enable wireless communication to rural areas by setting up wireless communication relay centres. With wireless communication, weather forecasts and innovations in agriculture practices can be relayed to farmers for them to cultivate their crops more effectively.

Second, 1.8 billion poor people in Asia who live on less than USD$2 a day are now able to gain access to microcredit through internet banking and mobile phone banking. Solar panels can now be found in most remote areas, including the highlands of the Himalayan Mountains.

Third, Asian companies are aware that having new products that are affordable by the huge market that consists of the low-income population can have good returns due to the economies of scale. A vast market makes it more attractive for them to innovate and find new ways of producing products that have lower cost of production. In addition, these products need to have a lower cost of maintenance when in use. Thus there is a huge amount of R&D effort to produce products that require lesser materials and energy. A good example is India's "Nano", an automobile developed and manufactured by Tata Company of India. The Basic Tata "Nano" car sells for about USD 2,484[13] (about Indian Rupee 115,361). The low-cost and fuel-efficient motor vehicle is perhaps one way to abate climate change by developed, emerging and developing nations.

Fourth, although Asian countries started industrialising at a later time, they are very aggressive in adopting new information

---

[13] Ex-show room price of Tata Nano in Delhi, http://tatanano.inservices. tatamotors.com/tatamotors/index.php?option=com_booking&task= pricelist&Itemid=303.

and communication technologies to leap-frog into the Information age. The penetration of broadband internet access in Asia is higher than in the USA. Currently, 95 percent of South Korean households and 88 percent of Singaporean households have broadband Internet access. In the USA, however, only 60 percent of households have broadband internet access.[14] The cause of this difference is due to the US having a legacy of land-line infrastructure that people have been dependent upon. Therefore, the shift to new technology is hindered. As many Asian countries do not have to deal with the legacy of huge land-based telecommunication infrastructure, they can start using the new wireless technology immediately.

Fifth, recent events in the Middle East and Thailand demonstrated the potential for the internet, mobile phones and social networking sites such as Facebook and Twitter. They are empowering the people to push for reform and democratic process, and governments will need to find innovative ways to meet their demands in order to retain their legitimacy. The democratic process will eventually lead to more entrepreneurial activities. New entrepreneurial activities can only result from new innovations.

The various forces of innovation are self-reinforcing and will create new impacts, especially in Asia. Moving forward with the rapid growth of R&D investments in Asia, we expect to see greater achievements from Asia in the coming decades.

Based on the World Intellectual Property Indicator 2009, the total number of patent applications from 2002 to 2006 submitted by leading countries in the field of technology showed that out of the total of 10.3 million patent applications, Asia Pacific countries submitted 5.1 million patents. The number of patents they submitted made up almost half of the world's submission during the four-year period (see Figure 2.3).

---

[14] According to the survey carried out by Strategy Analytics, USA, in June 2009.

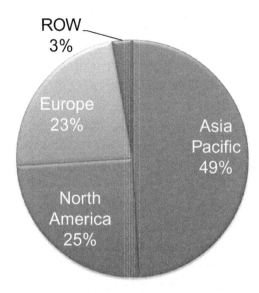

Figure 2.3: Patent applications by country of origin extracted from WIPO.[15]

Note: ROW means Rest of the World.

The three countries that submitted the most number of patent applications during the four-year period are Japan, South Korea and China. These three countries represented 48 percent of the number of patent applications in the world (see Table 2.2).

More inventions were made over the past 200 years than the other centuries before them (see Figure 2.4).

The blue light emitting diode (LED), which was invented by Shuji Nakajima from Japan in 1989, was an early indicator of the resurgence of Asia in today's modern world. In recognition of his contribution by Finland, he was awarded the 2006 Millennium Technology Prize.[16]

---

[15] World Intellectual Property Indicators 2009 by WIPO, Patents applications by field of technology (2002–2006 average) by leading countries. http://www.wipo.int/ipstats/en/statistics/patents/

[16] Source, http://www.millenniumprize.fi/index.php?page=2006-winner.

Table 2.2: Patent applications of top three Asia Pacific countries from 2002 to 2006 — represented almost half of the world's total patent applications.

Country	Number of Patent Applications (2002 to 2006 Total)	% of World Total
Japan	3,666,511	35%
South Korea	750,653	7%
China	515,092	5%
Top of Top Three Asia Pacific Countries	4,932,256	48%
Total in the World	10,334,468	

Source: WIPO Statistics Database, July 2009
Note: Country of Origin is the residence of the first-named applicant or assignee http://www.wipo.int/ipstats/en/statistics/patents/

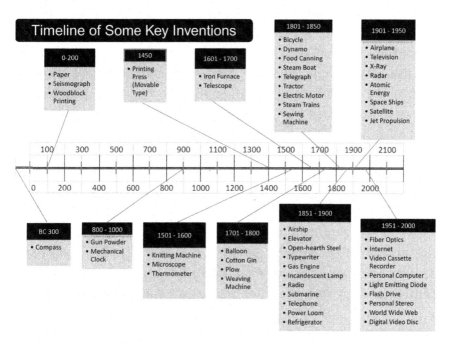

Figure 2.4: Time line of some key inventions.

25

Shuji Nakajima's breakthrough in high-output LEDs formed the basis for all high-capacity optical media. As many researchers around the world are also pursuing research in similar directions, and many researchers travel extensively to gain more scholarly interactions, it is likely that there will be parallel inventions or co-inventions. The main point in this section is to highlight how these inventions show that Asians are actively participating in pioneering research and breakthrough innovations.

A similar example of a breakthrough innovation is the flash memory stick (also known as thumb drive or flash memory) that we carry with us every day. This solid state electronic flash memory data storage device was invented by Professor Fujio Masuoka of Tohoku University in 1980. Today, it is used in digital cameras, handheld and mobile computers, mobile phones, music players, video game consoles and other electronic devices. Flash memory is considered to be the most important semiconductor innovation of the 1990s. Flash memory is a key technology that enables new designs for many computers and electronic devices sold in the market. According to iSuppli, the total nonvolatile memory market was worth US$ 22.5 billion in 2007 and will surpass US$ 37.7 billion by 2011.[17]

Another enabler or attraction that will sustain the rate of innovation in Asia Pacific is the human capital of talented researchers and the potential market that result from the large population of Asia Pacific.

If we were to map out the Asia Pacific geography, and take the ends of the Malacca Straits as a strategic sea lane connecting the two sides of Asia, using Singapore Airport as the centre, and lay out the flight time, we will see that within a

---

[17] Flash Memory Summit, Santa Clara, California, August 12–14, 2008, http://www.flashmemorysummit.com/English/Collaterals/Documents/FMS08_Press_Resource.pdf.

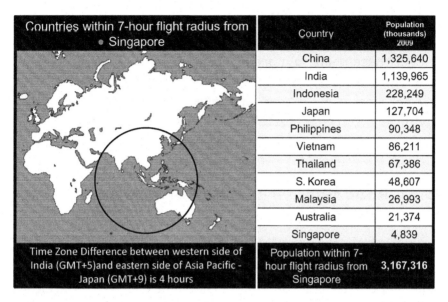

Countries within 7-hour flight radius from • Singapore	Country	Population (thousands) 2009
	China	1,325,640
	India	1,139,965
	Indonesia	228,249
	Japan	127,704
	Philippines	90,348
	Vietnam	86,211
	Thailand	67,386
	S. Korea	48,607
	Malaysia	26,993
	Australia	21,374
	Singapore	4,839
Time Zone Difference between western side of India (GMT+5)and eastern side of Asia Pacific - Japan (GMT+9) is 4 hours	Population within 7-hour flight radius from Singapore	3,167,316

Figure 2.5: Over three billion people live within seven-hour flight radius from Singapore. (Population Data from: 2009 World Population Data Sheet, Population Reference Bureau).

7-hour flight radius, over three billion people can be reached (see Figure 2.5).

With growing affluence, the potential market for products and services that incorporate new technologies and innovations will be very attractive for R&D investments.

A large pool of talented scientists and researchers will have no problem in having inter-disciplinary and cross-country collaboration. This is especially so in this era of budget air travel. The rapid growth of budget airlines makes air travel more affordable for all, especially researchers. Many educational institutions in India no longer consider going to Singapore as international travel. They treat their staff members who go to Singapore for academic purposes as domestic travel! With the time zone difference from the western side of India to the eastern side of Asia Pacific (Japan) being only four hours (see Figure 2.5), face-to-face interactions and telecommunication interactions can occur within the same daylight hours.

All these point to a great incentive for the research community to discuss and communicate amongst themselves. The ease of market access and large market size in Asia Pacific will continue to create sustainable momentum and be the key enabler for the transformation of innovative activities!

2.1 RESEARCH AND DEVELOPMENT INVESTMENTS

The pursuit of domestic and international R&D is becoming seamless as funding priorities shift towards Asia for global sourcing of ideas and solutions. The shift is driven by greater availability and lower cost of skilled and talented researchers. Moreover, governments and industries in Asia have made sustained aggressive investments in science and technology. The global R&D spending for the year 2009 (R&D Magazine and Battelle) is expected to reach US$ 1,143.2 billion. This is 3.2 percent higher than 2008.[18]

Most of the global growth is contributed by Asian countries (see Table 2.1). Asian governments continued investing in large amounts in R&D despite the current economic and financial crisis. Key government leaders in Asia Pacific believe that innovation is the key to economic growth and accelerated recovery from a downturn and thus are not cutting back on investment in R&D. Thriving multi-national enterprises understand that the continuing success of their business is largely dependent on continuous improvement and innovation. Gone are the days when products developed in home markets could be sold in other

---

[18] Page 3, Change Becomes Watchword for 2009's World of R&D, 2009 Global R&D Funding Forecast, Dec 2008, R&D Magazine.

markets. In order to penetrate the market and increase their market share, companies are delivering products according to local culture and needs.

With the increase in the wealth of Asian countries and to garner a bigger market share, multi-national enterprises are investing in local R&D to customise products to the markets they are serving. Both government spending and industry spending in R&D are contributing towards this growth of R&D spending in Asia Pacific in 2009.

Between 2004 and 2007, global multi-national enterprises located 83 percent of their new R&D sites in China and India.[19] In the same period, they increased their R&D staff by 22 percent, of which 91 percent of this increase was from China and India. This strongly indicated that China and India are preferred regions for their offshore R&D. This reinforces the fact that Asia now takes the lead with the highest R&D spending in the world.

The OECD Main Science Indicators provide us with more evidence of the increase of research intensity of Asia Pacific countries in comparison with the rest of the world (see Figure 2.6).

We will now examine the two most populous nations in Asia Pacific that have made significant increase in R&D investments, namely China and India.

China

China's R&D landscape has been transformed tremendously over the last decade, with its increasing emphasis on science and technology to drive economic growth. In 1996, China's investment in R&D was 0.6 percent of GDP; ten years later, in 2006,

---

[19] Page 55, *Beyond Borders: The Global Innovation 1000* by Barry Jaruzelski and Kenvin Dehoff, Booz & Co.

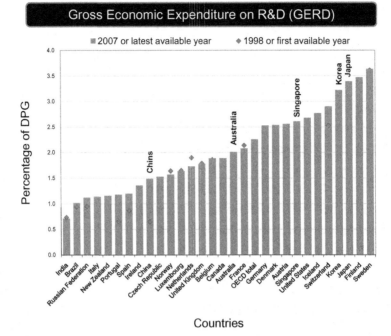

Figure 2.6: In Asia Pacific countries, including Japan, Korea, Singapore, Australia and China, R&D intensity has increased over the period of 1998 to 2006.[20]

Sources: OECD Factbook 2009: Economic, Environmental and Social Statistics; A*STAR Singapore

it increased to 1.6 percent of GDP. China's leadership continues to emphasise the role of R&D in building up the momentum of continued economic development. The Chinese government is emphasising the shift from agricultural and heavy industry to intensive knowledge-based industries. China's goal is to increase its R&D expenditure to 2 percent of GDP by 2010, and 2.5 percent by 2020. In addition, the globalisation and construction of

---

[20] OECD Factbook 2009: Economic, Environmental and Social Statistics, page 4; National Survey of R&D in Singapore in 2007, published by the Agency for Science, Technology and Research Singapore, December 2008; The Science & Technology Plan 2010, Ministry of Trade and Industry, Singapore, February 2006.

R&D centres across the world have contributed greatly to the growth of R&D investments in Asia Pacific, particularly in China and India.

Data from the OECD shows that China now ranks third worldwide in terms of the amount of GERD, just behind USA and Japan but ahead of the individual member states of the EU.

China's Rising Stature in Science and Technology

With the steep increase in R&D spending, China's research output has increased sharply over the past decade. In 2000, China's researchers published papers in the internationally influential science and social-science journals indexed by Thomson Reuters for its ISI Web of Science database which amounted to 3.9 percent of the world's output, compared to 9.9 percent in 2009.

Currently, China's biggest accomplishments are in the following fields:

- Material science
- Chemistry
- Physics
- Mathematics
- Engineering
- Computer science

Table 2.3 shows the percentage breakdown of the world's publication output in these fields from 2004 to 2008 (five years).

Citation impact relative to the world average has also increased, but not so significantly. In the area of physical science, the relative citation impact for China from 2004 to 2008 ranged from 68 percent to 90 percent of the world average, with engineering and mathematics at the top. Typically, output increases before a rise in impact is

Table 2.3: China's share of world publications in the top ranking of global share in the selected fields covered by Thomson Reuters.

Field	% of World Output	Ranking in Global Share of Publications
Material Science	21	1
Chemistry	17	2
Physics	14	3
Mathematics	13	4
Engineering	11	5
Computer Science	11	6

observed, as a developing nation builds a base with scientists, infrastructure and funding.

Thomson Reuters has recognised an increasing importance of China's research at the top end among well-known and highly cited research papers. Thomson Reuters' Essential Science Indicators database reveals that among the highly cited papers across all fields in the sciences and social sciences (top 1 percent in terms of citations, weighted for field and publication year), China represented 4.3 percent. This figure covers papers published from 1999 to 2008. China held a 7.3 percent share among "hot papers", which are defined as reports no more than two years old and are in the top 0.1 percent in terms of citations (again, weighted by field and publication date).

China aims to have its research recognised with a Nobel Prize. The trends outlined above and the appearance of more and more reports among the "hot" and highly cited papers in the physical sciences suggest that China might achieve its aim.

India

India focused more on science and technology initiatives by establishing many institutions devoted to science and higher education. It has national institutions devoted to different areas of research such as space, nuclear and IT. The number of Indian Institutes of Technology (IIT) between 1951 to 1963 was five; by 2008, there were 13 IITs.

The Prime Minister of India recently announced that India will increase investment in science and technology from the present 1 percent of Gross Domestic Product (GDP) to 2 percent over the next year or two. Like the National Science Foundation (NSF) in United States of America, the newly created National Science and Engineering Research Board in India will produce annual "science indicators" to drive research and measure yearly progress.

China and India — Research Output Has Been Rising Rapidly

The combined powerhouse of the two most populous nations is creating a new trend of a shift in the volume of publication output. The outcome resulting from their intensive investments in R&D is impressive. According to the Thomson Reuters Web of Knowledge Studies on China, the scientific research output had more than doubled since 2004. For India, the scientific research output had increased by 80 percent since 2000. This shift in the global arena shows both China and India making their impact felt in the areas of research and innovation. In the selected main fields, between China and India, they are within the top ten position of global share in 13 fields.

The 13 fields in which China and/or India are in the top ten position of global share are as follows:

1. Material Science (China being top one and India being top three of global share);
2. Chemistry (India being top one and China being top two of global share);

3. Physics (China being top three and India being top six of global share);
4. Mathematics (China being top four of global share);
5. Engineering (China being top five and India being top seven of global share);
6. Computer Science (China being top six of global share)
7. Geosciences (China being top seven and India being top eight of global share)
8. Pharmacology and Toxicology (India being top four and China being top eight of global share)
9. Environment/Ecology (China being top nine of global share)
10. Space Science (India being top nine and China being top ten of global share)
11. Agriculture Science (India being top two of global share)
12. Plant and Animal Science (India being top five of global share)
13. Microbiology (India being top ten of global share)

Table 2.4, collated by Thomson Reuters, provides details of growth and global share ranking of the 16 fields.

Korea

Korea's R&D output

The drive towards economic development and scientific achievement in Asia has spurred many Asian countries to invest heavily in education and technological innovations.

Korea's Science and Technology (S&T) Plan shares many similarities with that of Japan. Japan's high international competitiveness is due to the strong driving force in science and technology investments strategy. The Korean government further emphasized the importance of science and technology when they enacted legislation in September 2004 to promote the Minister of Science and Technology to the Deputy Prime

Table 2.4: Rising stature of China and India in global scientific output. Shows the top 16 global share ranking of China and India.

China and India's Share of World Publications in Selected Main Fields Covered by Thomson Reuters

	Field	Country	\multicolumn{2}{c}{1999-2003}		\multicolumn{3}{c}{2004-2008}	
			Count	Share (%)	Count	Share (%)	Global Share Ranking	Growth
1	Material Science	China	20,847	12.22	48,210	20.83	1	12
	Material Science	India	6,960	4.08	11,126	4.81	3	9
2	Chemistry	China	44,573	9.29	99,206	16.90	2	15
	Chemistry	India	22,206	4.42	33,504	5.70	1	10
3	Physics	China	31,103	7.97	66,153	14.16	3	17
	Physics	India	11,700	3.00	17,295	3.70	6	14
4	Mathematics	China	7,321	7.37	16,029	12.82	4	16
5	Engineering	China	19,343	6.42	43,162	10.92	5	14
	Engineering	India	8,101	2.69	14,103	3.57	7	5
6	Computer Science	China	3,943	4.54	16,009	10.66	6	4
7	Geosciences	China	5,322	4.95	12,673	9.30	7	11
	Geosciences	India	2,839	2.64	4,266	3.13	8	13
8	Pharmacology & Toxicology	China	2,259	3.11	6,614	7.28	8	7
	Pharmacology & Toxicology	India	2,034	2.80	3,866	4.25	4	3
9	Environment/Ecology	China	3,171	3.26	9,032	6.85	9	8
10	Space Science	China	2,055	3.8	3,514	5.89	10	21
	Space Science	India	1,322	2.44	1,665	2.79	9	18
11	Agriculture Science	China	1,082	1.48	4,872	4.88	13	1
	Agriculture Science	India	4,303	5.91	5,634	5.65	2	17
12	Plant & Animal Science	China	5,915	2.61	14,646	5.42	12	9
	Plant & Animal Science	India	8,132	3.58	10,190	3.77	5	19
13	Biology & Biochemistry	China	6,697	2.66	15,971	5.86	11	10
14	Microbiology	China	921	1.38	3,863	4.74	14	3
	Microbiology	India	1,078	1.62	2,273	2.79	10	2
15	Molecular Biology & Genetics	China	1,642	1.43	6,210	4.49	15	5
16	Immunology	China	493	0.87	2,114	3.51	16	2

Source: Thomson Reuters: Global Research Report — China and Global Research Report — India.[21]

---

[21] Global Research Report — China, Jonathan Adams, Christopher King, Nan Ma, Nov 2009, Thomson Reuters; Global Research Report — India, Jonathan Adams, Christopher King, Vinay Singh, Thomson Reuters.

Minister level. In addition to the current responsibilities of planning, coordination and evaluation of S&T related policies, the Minister will also coordinate and allocate national R&D programs.

Korea's S&T vision for 2025 is to reach the following goals:

1. $80 billion for R&D expenditure
2. 314,000 R&D Personnel
3. 30 percent S&T contribution to economic growth

Korea's continued focus on investments in R&D is reflected by the high percentage of Gross Economic Expenditure on R&D (GERD) — from 2.34% GERD in 1998 to 3.22% in 2007 (see Figure 2.6).

Singapore

Singapore is another country that is changing the research landscape in Asia. Singapore has been intensifying its R&D activities to transform its capital-intensive economy in the 1980s to a knowledge- and innovation-intensive economy in the 2000s (see Figure 2.7).

For example, the overall R&D expenditure was increased from S$5 billion in 2006 to S$6.3 billion in 2007, a hefty 26 percent increase. As a percentage of GDP, the GERD increased from 2.31 percent to 2.61 percent in 2007. Singapore's strategic goal is to go beyond 3% GERD by the year 2015.

Singapore's science and technology investment with a GERD level of 2.61 percent compares very favourably with the key economies of the world. At 2.61 percent, it is approaching that of the USA (2.68 percent in 2007), and is above the OECD countries' average of 2.26 percent in 2006.

With the rapid increase in research intensity, Singapore's biomedical, pharmaceutical, clean energy, water reuse and management, information and media communication industries are expected to have a sustainable pipeline of new knowledge and

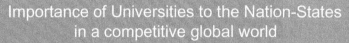

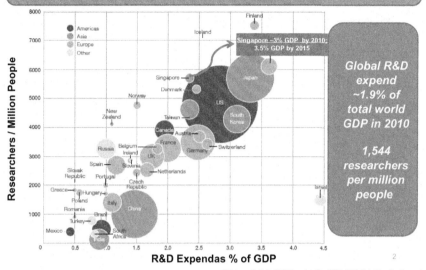

Reference: Battelle, R&D Magazine, Dec 2009 : 2010 Global Funding Forecast

Figure 2.7: Singapore's strategic R&D investments towards a knowledge and innovation-intensive economy.

innovation to add value to the economic development of Singapore and to have a spillover effect on the Asia Pacific region.

Key Innovation Outcome of Some Asian Countries

Many Asian governments are embracing innovation as their key national and global agenda. Based on studies by INSEAD, four Asian countries feature among the top-10 of the Global Innovation Index rankings (Figure 2.8).

Korea and China have three digit percentage increases in the number of patent applications being filed (see Figure 2.9).

In 2002, 312,000 patents were granted around the world. 146,000 patents were granted to Asia Pacific, 88,000 patents to North America and 56,000 patents to Europe (see Figure 2.10).

37

Changing Research Landscape

Driving Forces of Global Innovation
• Innovation as a National & Global Agenda

Key Innovation Outcome of Some Asian Countries

Country/ Economy	Global Innovation Index Rankings		
	2011	2010	2009
Switzerland	1	4	7
Sweden	2	2	3
Singapore	3	7	5
Hong Kong (SAR), China	4	3	12
Finland	5	6	13
Denmark	6	5	8
USA	7	11	1
Canada	8	12	11
Netherlands	9	8	10
United Kingdom	10	14	4
South Korea	16	20	6
Japan	20	13	9
China *	29	43	37

Note: * China is moving up the ranking very quickly

Source: The Global Innovation Index 2011, Soumitra Dutta, INSEAD

Singapore
(in top 10 for 3 years)
2009 - #5; 2010 - #7; 2011-#3

Hong Kong
(in top 10 for 2 years)
2010 - #3; 2011-#4

South Korea
(in top 10 for 1 year)
2009-#6

Japan
(in top 10 for 1 year)
2009-#9

Figure 2.8: Key innovation outcome of some Asian countries. Singapore is in the top 10 of the global innovation index rankings for the last 3 Years.

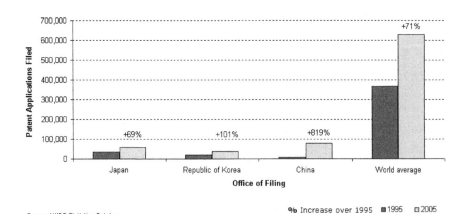

Source: WIPO Statistics Database

% Increase over 1995 ■ 1995 □ 2005

Figure 2.9: Patent applications filed by Japan, South Korea and China.

38

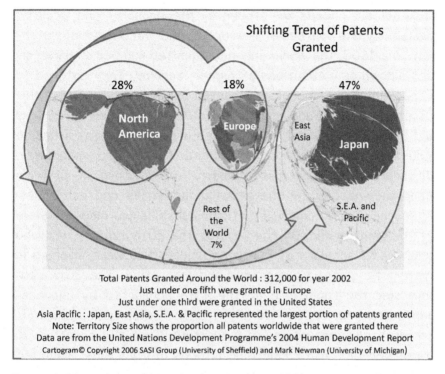

Figure 2.10: The world patent distribution in 2002 — Strong indication of the shifting share of patents towards Asia Pacific.

The internationalisation of R&D and the strategic thrust of most Asia Pacific countries desiring high-tech industries with high R&D investments growth in Asia Pacific over the past years have resulted in the increase in both publications and patents from Asia Pacific countries. The changing face of innovation and the shift of innovations towards Asia Pacific is happening!

2.2 UNIVERSITIES

The role of universities has evolved over the centuries. These changes resulted from shifts in the expectations of stakeholders, needs of students, the economy and society, availability and sources of resources, and the degree of autonomy. Pre-1600, the world only had a limited number of universities, known as institutions of higher learning. They catered to a special group of people interested in the arts, theology, philosophy, medicine and law. Post-1600s, several new inventions and large scale shifts in Western Europe from agriculture to industrialisation spurred the need for skilled manpower. Universities and specialised institutions stepped in to train manpower needed by the growing industries and economies. Widespread dissemination of technical skills was made possible by the print media. By the turn of the 20th century, growing numbers of scholars at European universities were involved in systematic scientific research and innovation. The 20th century saw the rapid rise of the USA supported by unprecedented expansion of its university sector and scientific research and innovation-led industries. Over the past two to three decades, many emerging nations of Asia have emulated the success of the USA and expanded their university sector and pool of scientific researchers. Moreover, the digital media and internet catalysed the transformation of Asia. Asian universities have been given greater autonomy in governance and resources, and in the process education, research and enterprise have become the key missions of several universities. Asian universities are now competing for talented students and academics. An outcome of these developments is that the scientific research and innovation community is now globally dispersed. With the advent of digitisation of information and speed of communication, the dissemination of new knowledge and innovation hastened. With the ability to communicate speedily and effectively, the research community around the world is increasingly internationalised and integrated.

Many universities have also opened their doors for international students. According to an estimate, there are now more

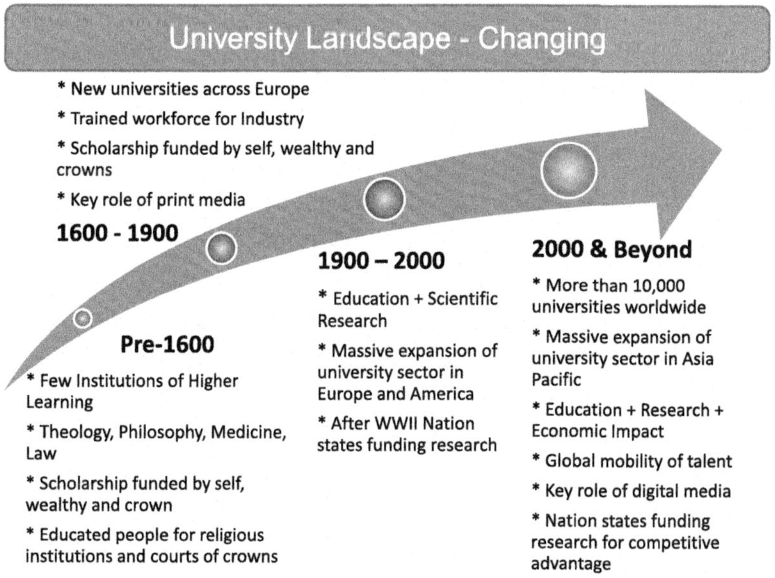

University Landscape - Changing

* New universities across Europe

* Trained workforce for Industry

* Scholarship funded by self, wealthy and crowns

* Key role of print media

1600 - 1900

1900 – 2000

* Education + Scientific Research

* Massive expansion of university sector in Europe and America

* After WWII Nation states funding research

Pre-1600

* Few Institutions of Higher Learning

* Theology, Philosophy, Medicine, Law

* Scholarship funded by self, wealthy and crown

* Educated people for religious institutions and courts of crowns

2000 & Beyond

* More than 10,000 universities worldwide

* Massive expansion of university sector in Asia Pacific

* Education + Research + Economic Impact

* Global mobility of talent

* Key role of digital media

* Nation states funding research for competitive advantage

Figure 2.11: The changing role of universities from local to regional to globalization of education and research in less than five decades!

than three million international students, and the number is likely to grow by 5 percent.

The global mobility of students and academics gave rise to the new phenomenon of global benchmarking of universities by several organisations such as:

* Times Higher Education — QS World University Rankings.[22]
* The Academic Ranking of World Universities compiled by Shanghai Jiao Tong University, China (http://www.arwu.org/)
* Taiwan HEEC (http://ranking.heeact.edu.tw/en-us/2009/TOP/100)

---

[22] After the 2009 rankings, Times Higher Education ended their relationship with QS and worked with Thomson Reuters to provide data for its annual world university rankings. From Nov 2010, QS Quacquarelli Symonds will continue to produce the World University Rankings using data collected and analysed over the past six years by itself and SCOPUS by Elsevier.

- U.S. News & World Report College and University Rankings (http://colleges.usnews.rankingsandreviews.com/best-colleges)

Although there are ongoing debates on the value, criteria and assumptions used in the ranking process, the ranking of universities is driving competition amongst universities towards global excellence.

The interest in knowing how universities are ranked is high as demonstrated by the high number of visits to the Times-QS website. On 1st November 2009, Google Analytics[23] tracked a total number of five million web visitors to the QS World University Rankings website, www.topuniversities.com.

1.6 million web visitors were from Asia Pacific, representing 45 percent of the top 25 countries (see Figure 2.12 and Table 2.5).

The pie chart shows that people in Asia Pacific have the highest interest in knowing how universities are ranked. We can easily deduce that a big portion would be potential students/parents who are deciding which universities to choose for their tertiary studies. Another group would be university researchers looking for collaborators. Another key group would be government agencies wanting to know how their countries' universities are benchmarked against other countries.

In the future, research-intensive universities will become more international. This means that the community of students, faculty and researchers will include a diversity of local and overseas personnel. In addition, research and teaching collaborations will see the exchange of students and staff across borders.

---

[23] http://www.topuniversities.com/articles/rankings/qs-world-university-rankings-reaches-5-million-web-visitors-topuniversities.com, accessed on 5/31/2010 4:24 PM.

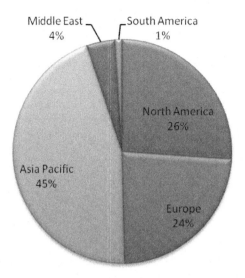

Figure 2.12: Pie chart of annual number of web visitors to topuniversities.com from the top 25 countries as of 1st November 2009.

Source: http://www.topuniversities.com/articles/rankings/qs-world-university-rankings-reaches-5-million-web-visitors-topuniversities.com.

Singapore

"Scientific breakthroughs were often not made by single brilliant researchers working in isolation" — Prime Minister of Singapore Lee Hsien Loong.[24]

The Singapore government firmly believes in having a comprehensive approach to investing in its people at all levels. As Singapore continues to expand its knowledge and innovation-intensive economy, research-intensive universities become the engine for creating new knowledge to sustain economic and social developments as well as to help society to prosper. This will also help the nation to remain competitive in the globalised world (see Figure 2.13).

---

[24] Addendum to President's address: Research funding to continue (22 May 2009), *The Straits Times.*

Table 2.5: Shows the number of website visitors from various countries.

Annual Number of Rankings Visitors to topUniversities.com — Top 25 Countries

Country	Number of Visits
United States	775,946
United Kingdom	534,389
India	275,562
Canada	239,463
Singapore	194,099
Japan	192,294
Malaysia	167,813
Pakistan	148,374
Australia	145,890
Hong Kong	127,141
China	116,409
Iran	113,594
South Korea	96,304
Germany	90,226
Indonesia	86,213
Thailand	81,972
Italy	74,584
Taiwan	67,996
Netherlands	57,383
Turkey	57,151
Philippines	56,099
Saudi Arabia	51,390
France	49,807
Greece	48,724
Mexico	39,346
Sub-total of Web visitors from Top 25 countries	3,888,169
Rest of the World	1,111,831
Total Web Visitors	5,000,000

All Asia Pacific countries are in various phases of moving towards a knowledge-intensive economy. The emphasis on building a pool of highly-trained and skilled workers to conduct R&D is building up momentum.

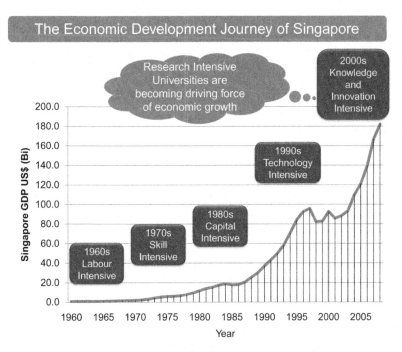

Figure 2.13: The economic development journey of Singapore.
Source: Singapore Department of Statistics

The growth of Asia Pacific universities is already taking place and they are challenged to join the global league of top universities.

The analysis of the top 50 universities in the world shows more Asia Pacific universities gaining recognition.

Analysis of the top 50 universities based on The QS Top Universities World Ranking for year 2008 and 2009 yielded the following results (see Table 2.6).

Asia Pacific universities have caught up with European universities in terms of the number of world-class universities. Our mothers often imbue in children, "Education is the key to your future success." Government leaders in Asia place great value in education. They see universities as strategic resources that are fundamental to the progress of their countries. As

Table 2.6: Asia Pacific universities comprised about one-third of the top 50 universities in the world.

Region	2008		2009	
	No. of Universities in the Top 50	% of Universities in the Top 50	No. of Universities in theTop 50	% of Universities in the Top 50
North America (incl Canada)	23	44%	21	42%
Asia Pacific (incl Australia & NZ)	15	29%	15	30%
Europe	14	27%	14	28%
Note: There was a tie among three universities for the 50th position in 2008.				

family values and government values are in sync, great strides are being made to promote education.

With increased access and focus on tertiary education, Asia Pacific universities are seen as research engines vital to producing new knowledge and driving innovations. Another dimension has since been added to universities to incubate and drive the entrepreneurial spirit of nations with the innovation and new knowledge they have generated. This means that universities are not just a source of highly skilled manpower, but also a place to groom a new pool of talent that will become future entrepreneurs and employers who will create more new jobs for society.

Current State of Higher Education

In USA, there are more undergraduates taking up other disciplines of studies besides natural science and engineering. Table 2.7 shows that Singapore has the highest percentage of undergraduates pursuing natural science or engineering. Of the top five countries, China ranked second and USA ranked fifth. In terms of percentage, China has more number of undergraduates taking up natural science and engineering courses, compared to those in USA.

Table 2.7 Percentage of all undergraduates with degrees in Natural Science or Engineering.

Country	% of all undergraduate with degrees in Natural Science or Engineering
Singapore	67%
China	50%
France	47%
South Korea	38%
USA	15%

Source: NSF

There had been various debates on the comparable estimate of the number of graduating engineers with four-year degree courses from China and the United States.

One of the most conservative estimates based on a comparable four-year degree course concluded that China produced about 350,000 science and engineering graduates whereas United States produced about 140,000 science and engineering graduates in year 2004. China, has therefore, produced 2.5 times more engineering and science graduates than USA has done.

In spring 2010, OECD reported that throughout Europe, the recent financial crisis saw reduction in higher education spendings. This varied anywhere between 10 percent to 50 percent. The reduction in universities funding was 50 percent for universities in Latvia and 10 percent in Ireland. Britain decreased its university funding by 450 million sterling pounds. France and Germany have not reduced university spending. In the case of France, an increase in spending depends on whether an increase in borrowing can be obtained. In the case of Germany, funding proposals for gifted programs and selected professions will be reviewed; there will be no increase in core funding.

The decrease in funding for university education in Europe is unsettling and the Head of Department of Education, OECD commented that, "*I am not sure whether the countries that have the strongest higher education systems today will still have them ten years from now.*"

With these changes in tertiary education in both the USA and Europe, one will see a growing shift in the number of researchers from the USA and Europe to Asia Pacific countries.

Geographic Distribution of Researchers in the World

Various global reports on doctorate studies in science and engineering indicated that an increasing number of non-citizens are completing their doctorate in engineering, mathematics and computer science in their host countries. A big proportion of these non-citizen doctorates are from the Asia Pacific region.

Table 2.8 shows that the percentage of non-USA citizens in USA universities pursuing a doctoral degree in natural science, including physical, biological, earth, ocean and atmospheric sciences and engineering is very significant, especially for engineering.

Table 2.9 shows that of all the foreign students pursuing doctorate programs, about half of them are from Asia. As many of these doctorates continued to stay in the USA, it was reported that in the year 2000, the USA science and technology workforce had 38 percent of PhDs who were from foreign countries.

Table 2.8: Doctoral degrees: percentage of foreign students in USA universities.

Doctoral degree in Natural Science (including the physical, biological, earth, ocean and atmospheric sciences	Percentage of foreign students in a USA university: 34
Doctoral degree in Engineering	Percentage of foreign students in a USA university: 56

Source: NSF

Table 2.9: Number of Non-USA citizens earning doctorate degrees from USA Institutions. 2006 report by NSF, Division of Science Resource Statistics.

Non-U.S. citizens from Countries Pursuing Science and Engineering Doctorates at USA Institutions (2006 Report)

China*	4,323	27.1
India	1,524	9.6
South Korea	1,219	7.6
Taiwan	431	2.7
Canada	363	2.3
Turkey	357	2.2
Russia	223	1.4
Japan	222	1.4
Thailand	199	1.2
Romania	187	1.2
All Others**	6,899	43.3
	15,947	100.0

*Includes Hong Kong.
**Includes non-USA citizens from all other countries
Source: National Science Foundation, Division of Science Resource Statistics

There is an overall growth in science and engineering capacity globally, and Asia Pacific is making a significant contribution in this area.

This trend is seen in the recent UNESCO Institute of Statistic report under: the Global Perspective of Distribution of Researchers in the World.

As seen in Table 2.10, the growing pie of researchers in Asia Pacific indicated that in each year, the number of graduates who pursue doctorate degrees and take up research positions at universities in Asia is significant enough.

From Table 2.9, we can see that the large number of Asian doctorate students could be a potential resource that Asian countries can draw upon to establish research centres or

Table 2.10: Geographic distribution of researchers in the world (2002 and 2007).

Geographic Distributions of Researchers in the World			
Region	2002	2007	Trend
Asia Pacific	35.7	41.4	Increase
Europe	31.9	28.4	Decrease
North America	25.2	22.2	Decrease
Latin America	2.9	3.6	Increase
Africa	2.3	2.3	No change
Middle East	2.0	2.1	Increase

Source: A Global Perspective on Research and Development, UIS Fact Sheet, October 2009, no. 2, UNESCO Institute for Statistics

conduct research. In addition to the foreign-trained pool of talents, Asian countries are also training more and more engineers and scientists in their local universities.

With a higher emphasis on science and engineering, human capital and capacity will be the enabling factor for more global collaborations in research and development.

Scientific Publications

China's aggressive investment in university education and research and development over the past decade is making a significant contribution towards new knowledge as seen in the increase in scientific publications. According to the Thomson Reuters Global Research Report on China, 2006 was a pivotal year for China. During this year, the total number of scientific publications surpassed that of Germany and Japan (see Figure 2.14). For the first time, China was ranked as the second and the USA was ranked as first in the area of scientific publications.

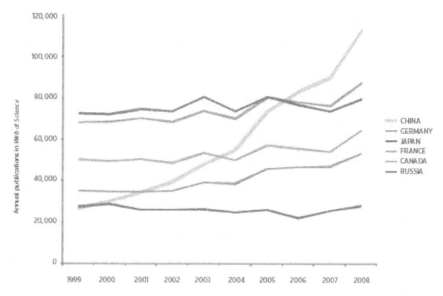

Figure 2.14: Annual publications in the Web of Science from 1999 to 2008.
(Not shown on the graph is that USA publications in 1999 was 265,000 and in 2008 was 340,000.)
Source: Thomson Reuters

China had a humble start of only 20,000 scientific papers in 1998 as recorded in the Thomson Reuters Web of Science database. In 2008, it published 112,000 scientific papers — a 460% increase in the number of papers published 10 years ago. During the same period, USA scientific publication increased from 265,000 to 340,000, a growth of 28 percent (see Figure 2.14). China continued to be ranked second in the world in 2008 in terms of the total number of scientific publications and USA continued to be ranked first.

Universities will continue to be the centres of new knowledge generation and the cornerstone for nations' social development, economic growth, environmental sustainability and well-being of mankind. In today's globalised world, key Asia

Pacific universities that desire to become global contributors to society have or are starting to put in place key strategic thrusts along the following lines:

- Internationalisation of faculties, researchers and students;
- Global and regional partnerships in education and research;
- Investment in research infrastructure to attract global institution partners, government and industries to work as a community;
- Promotion of collaborations amongst university, policy makers and industries;
- Adoption of a multi-disciplinary approach in research that focus on both national and global challenges.

All these initiatives point to the important role that global universities will continue to play.

2.3 YOUNG MINDS AND HUMAN RESOURCES

The interest to pursue science and engineering and advanced studies varies with different regions of the world.

As we advance towards the information- and knowledge-intensive society of the 21st century, the nurturing of future human capital becomes critical.

By 2050, there will be about 1.2 billion youths (see Figure 2.15), and most of them will be moving to urban cities. We need to create opportunities to develop these young minds.

China is focusing on developing young minds by making education available to all. The country is expecting highly-educated citizens to upgrade its economy beyond basic manufacturing to tertiary industries. Its universities have boosted enrolment by as much as 30 percent a year over the last decade, reaching 21.5 million in 2008.

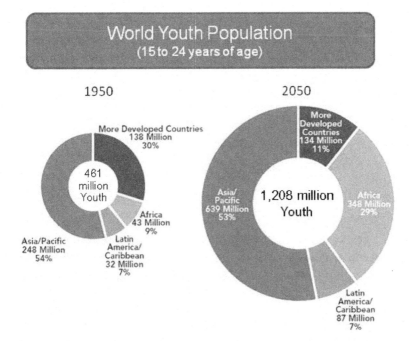

Figure 2.15: World youth population. It is estimated that a higher proportion of young people (ages 15 to 24) will reside in Africa and Asia Pacific by 2050.

Source: UN Population Division, World Population Prospects: The 2008 revision, medium variant (2009)

According to an article in *Newsweek* dated 8 September 2008, 90 percent of all engineers will be in Asia by 2011.

Tertiary education spending is growing globally. Between 1990 and 2001, 135 of 200 territories in the world have increased spending in tertiary education. There was a huge increase in the amount of spending.

As of 18 July 2009:

- Over 50 percent of world population is under 25 years old (UNFPA)
- Youths feel an obligation to act, so solving problems through business makes sense to them.

- The 1.2 billion people arriving in the workforce by 2050 will all be young and they will need challenging and meaningful work. We will need to educate and groom these young minds to reach their full potential. A big portion of them will be able to invent and discover new things for the betterment of mankind.

State of China and India

China and India have a new generation of young and talented scientists and engineers who have imbibed the entrepreneurial spirit. These young talents are more adventurous and risk-oriented in trying their technology-based ideas in the markets. Some notable examples are Mr. Jack Ma who started Alibaba Group[25] in 1999 when he was 35 years old and another group of seven entrepreneurs from India who started Infosys Technologies[26] in 1981. N.R. Narayana Murthy, the Founder-Chairman of Infosys Technologies, was also 35 years old when the company was formed in 1981. The co-founder, Mr. Nandan M. Nilekani, was then 26 years old.

China's and India's Intellectual Diaspora — Reverse Brain-drain

The dream of many young scientists and engineers from China and India is to do their post-graduate studies in the USA or Europe. This trend started in the 1960s and still continues. In the past, many of them remained in their home country after their studies.

---

[25] Alibaba Group — www.alibaba.com.
[26] Infosys — http://www.infosys.com.

China's Intellectual Diaspora — Reverse Brain-drain

In the late 1990s, young talents went overseas to seek academic opportunities and only a small percentage of them returned to China. Those who returned were often sponsored by the government and returned to serve their bond. With the rapid economic growth in China in the 2000s, an increasing number of returnees are making use of opportunities that arise from rapid economic growth.

India's Intellectual Diaspora — Reverse Brain-drain

In India, the expanding economy, a steady increase in young talented people, opening up of the society and strengthening of innovation initiatives and activities will continue to build up the momentum for contributing new knowledge and innovations to meet both national and global societal challenges.

Despite serious issues such as massive poverty and environmental problems, India's young people continue to aspire to focus on high standards of education and are ready to participate and fit into the global pool of top-class researchers.

A unique feature of innovation initiatives in India is that they are highly dependent on the international networks of Indians abroad working for multi-national enterprises or as academics. These networks bring young and bright talents into their "circle of research".

There are around 20 million "Global Indians" living outside India, travelling widely and having strong links within the innovation network. While most countries rely on an innovation system that links research to business, India relies a great deal on an innovation cadre — a diaspora of global Indians. This group has an important role in driving innovation in India and will continue to grow.

There is little doubt that China at present has a big edge over India as China has a greater advantage in advanced technology in terms of its sheer volume of products and the amount of foreign direct investment. However, India is catching up with its demographic advantage in the coming years. China's one-child policy versus India's current population growth will lead to the scenario where India will have a higher percentage of young people in the second half of the 21st century.

Shifting Focus from Asia Pacific to Global Research Foundation

The shift to Asia Pacific is occurring now and it has human resources to sustain the momentum of the shift with a growing younger population.

If we combine the two "giants", the growing number of young talented people will provide the human resources to continue and maintain the increasing trend of innovation efforts in Asia Pacific. The "pipeline" of young minds in China and India will be sustainable in the 21st century in providing the human capital for continuing research and development efforts.

China has a higher percentage of university-educated workers than European countries such as Germany. Germany has 20 percent while China has 33 percent of university-educated workers.

The human resources or human capital that China and India can count on for sustainable research and development will come from four major sources.

The first will be scientists and scholars who return to their home country.

Second will be the travelling scientists and scholars from their adopted base (USA or Europe) to China or India for collaboration or entrepreneurial projects.

Third will be the young and talented local scientists and scholars who are currently being trained.

Fourth is the increased entry and retention of women in the research community who will make important contributions towards the talent pool. More and more women are attaining higher levels of education thus contributing towards a sustainable pool of talent for the global research community.

These pipelines of talent can be great sources for global research initiatives or projects. We recommend the implementation of a Global Research Foundation to facilitate a global research community with shared vision, responsibilities and research data that can tap on these pipeline of talents to find solutions for global societal challenges. We envisage global research teams comprising researchers from several nations and disciplines working together and focusing on specific ways of addressing global challenges. With these efforts, the duplication of research will be reduced and there will be better use of funds. The future will become a better place for more collaboration and less competition for funding.

2.4 OPENNESS AND BROADER ACCESS TO KNOWLEDGE

The openness and wider access to knowledge via the internet, mobile phones and satellite television is raising awareness of new knowledge and intellect around the world.

When handwritten manuscripts were the only way of exchanging information and knowledge, access to information and knowledge was limited to a small number of people in society. The speed of such access was dependent on the speed of the completion of a single copy manuscript and the mode of transportation for the delivery of manuscripts. The transfer of knowledge was limited to an elite and small group of intellectuals.

The invention of paper, block and movable type printing enabled better distribution of information as people were able to make multiple copies through printing. The speed of distribution was still hindered by the mode of transportation through which the printed material was delivered. With the invention of printing press in 1440 by Johannes Gutenberg from Germany, printed books were made available to all. This led to the spreading of knowledge related to technological developments in Europe with an unprecedented speed. It was the rapid and wider access to information that fuelled the industrial revolution in Europe.

The print media, radio and television primarily supported one-way communications. The information is disseminated to many locations, from one source out to many people who can read, listen or watch in a passive manner.

The advent of the internet changed the way we communicate and opened up a much wider means for dissemination of information and knowledge. With the internet, several people are able to communicate simultaneously and interactively. The internet allows a huge community of people to have two-way communication. The communities range from a few to millions of people, and they share information and knowledge round the clock, 365 days a year. The internet enables an easier and broader exchange of information and knowledge. This allows researchers and educators to play a more active role and influence outcome within a shorter time. In addition, instantaneous peer reviews and debates can be conducted across borders and different time zones. The key implication is that scientific and knowledge-based communication can be done simultaneously across national and institutional boundaries.

Internet is the key enabler of globalisation. The widening, deepening and speeding up of connectedness through the internet on a local, regional and global scales has made the world a "global village". The traditional role of libraries being "warehouses" of printed material is undergoing a transformational change. Many libraries around the world are now advocating open access to publications for the global community of researchers. The open online access to libraries' digital repositories will facilitate research on a global scale and herald great opportunities for international collaborations.

Some websites provide print books and publications for free online, e.g. the Gutenberg Project. Today, one can download over 30,000 free e-books from the Gutenburg Project website[27] to read on our personal computers and portable devices such as Kindle, Sony Reader, iPhones and iPads.

Asia Pacific countries understand that the internet and associated telecommunication technologies can be utilised to quicken their socio-economic developments into a new era of the knowledge-intensive economy.

Higher Education is Leveraging on the Internet

With openness and broader access to information via the internet, major universities are also now testing or implementing web-based education and using internet tools in combination with telephony and video to reach out within their own community and the outside world.

Many established universities are providing free and open access to college level lectures and courses. The following examples illustrate the increasing openness and broader access to information for all people who have internet access.

Academic Earth (http://academicearth.org/) was founded by Richard Ludlow. Its mission is to provide everyone with the opportunity to receive a world-class education

---

[27] http://www.gutenberg.org.

by inviting some of the world's top scholars and researchers to teach via the internet. Academic Earth leverages on the internet and associated technology to provide better access and ease of learning. Today, there are over 400 world-class lecturers providing free online video courses from leading universities including Berkeley, Columbia, Harvard, MIT, NYU, Princeton, Stanford, UCLA and Yale. Over 21 subjects that range from science and engineering, social sciences and humanities at university course level are provided for free through the internet.

TED (http://www.ted.com/) was established as a non-profit organisation in 1996 by Chris Anderson. The goal of TED is to foster great ideas. TED's mission is to spread good thinking globally and it aims to reach around 4.5 billion people who do not speak English. It uses its website as a platform to share ideas with anyone who has internet access. To allow more people who speak different languages to learn, the free videos are translated into 40 different languages.

YouTube EDU (http://www.youtube.com/education) is another platform used by more than a hundred universities to have access to their lectures and courses. The National University of Singapore (NUS), which is ranked among the top global universities, started to use YouTube as a video channel to share popular campus discussions in 2008. The website, http://www.youtube.com/nuscast, allows people to upload and view videos online. YouTube EDU currently has more than 200 full courses available on the internet.

Research Databases — The International Human Genome Project

The International Human Genome Project is an excellent example of a large-scale virtual collaboration. The GenBank databases that store information about the sequence of the human DNA are located in the USA (National Center for Biotechnology Information), Europe and Japan. GenBank is available to anyone who has internet access. This has given a major impetus to scientific work in recent years. The GenBank was a result of collaboration within an international virtual research consortium with geneticists from the USA, the UK, France, Germany, Japan, China and India. This $3 billion project started in 1990 and was completed in 2003, two years ahead of schedule. This was largely due to major advances in computer technology and better access and connectivity to the internet. The philosophy of openness and sharing to conduct collaborative global research of this magnitude benefited the global research community. The internet and network of global researchers will be key enablers for the furtherance of innovation to meet global challenges.

As of July 2009, China has 338 million internet users. The number of internet users in China is greater than the total population of the USA. The number of broadband internet users will continue to increase rapidly as China improves its rural coverage. Currently, about 95 percent of townships are connected to broadband and 92.5 percent of villages have telephone lines that can be used for internet access. China has embarked on the creation of a 3G network which will increase speed and coverage.

The growing web population has helped over 28 percent of web users to gain better scope and access to knowledge. This will in turn spur more innovations from a larger population.

This connectedness and mobility are key factors that are leading to more open and broader access to knowledge and information. This is one key enabler that is causing the geographical shift of innovation from Atlantic to Pacific.

2.5   OPEN INNOVATION PRACTICES OF COMPANIES

The concept of open innovation was first developed by Henry Chesbrough.[28]

Major companies have been investing about one to five percent of their revenues to support in-house research and product development mainly to improve their product lines and markets. In recent years, there is growing research and development activity around the world primarily fueled by funding from national governments to promote economic growth and employment creation.

Companies have come to realise that they no longer have all the answers, they cannot employ all the talent they would like to have, and they are better placed to tap into research and innovations happening outside their companies so that they can serve their markets and customers with more innovative products and compete effectively. Big companies such as GE, IBM, HP, Intel, Nokia, Proctor & Gamble, BASF and Philips have been practicing open innovation models by leveraging on leading researchers from universities and research institutes around the world. Even the highly protective pharmaceutical industry is showing signs of embracing open innovation models.

Some key examples in the following section describe this trend and how the company's focus is shifting to Asia Pacific.

Indian engineering services exports jumped by 25.6 percent in 2008.[29] Global car manufacturers such as Ford, GM, Chrysler

---

[28] Prof Henry Chesbrough, http://www2.haas.berkeley.edu/Faculty/chesbrough_henry.aspx.

[29] Engineering services exports jumps 25.6 percent in FY08 (16 August). *Business Standard, India, http://www.business-standard.com/india/storypage.php?autono=331537.*

Honda, and Volkswagen have set up engineering design centers in India.

The automobile industry is characterised by constant innovations to meet the changing tastes and needs of consumers for motorised transportation. The automobile industry accounts for about 17 percent of global research and development expenditure.

The first car was built in Germany 130 years ago (in 1879), and patented by Karl Benz of Mercedes-Benz (German Patent DRP No. 37435). A majority of their innovations were done in their in-house facilities. This is, however, changing. Daimler, the manufacturer of Mercedes-Benz, has started their "Open Innovation Network". This is to enable their own employees and selected external partners to contribute new and creative ideas that will lead to new technologies and products.

Ford came up with the mass production of cars in the early 1990s.

Toyota Company's investment to bring out an eco-friendly car has resulted in a car powered by solar panels. This innovation is covered by 1,000 patents worldwide.

Here is an overview of how the shift in automobile innovations had moved from the Atlantic to the Pacific in recent years (see Figure 2.16).

In 2007, the top research and development spender was Toyota. Toyota spent US$8.39 billion on research and development or 3.6 percent of global sales. Research and development was up by 7.6 percent from 2006, and Toyota was also the first on the list.

In the automobile industry, Asia's automakers spent 4.65 billion dollars more than those in USA did and 4.33 billion dollars more than those in Europe did. Asia's automakers spent over 20 percent more than their counterparts in Europe or USA (see Table 2.12).

Philips established its Open Innovation Campus in Shanghai, China in August 2007 with two key objectives. The first

130 years of Innovations in Automobile Industry
Shift from Atlantic to Pacific

Japan - Toyota Company
Solar Panel-Powered PRIUS 2009
Covered by 1000 patents worldwide

Germany - Karl Benz
first automobile in
1879

During the interim
period: Asian
automakers had
overtaken Europe and
USA in number of
innovations and
productions of cars in
the global market

India – Tata
Nano – World's Cheapest Car

1879

2009

USA – Ford Company
Model T - 1909

China – BYD China Auto
Dec 2008 - first mass produced plug-in
hybrid car in China

Figure 2.16: Shift in innovation of automobiles from Atlantic to Pacific.

Table 2.11: Car industry research and development spending.

Company	Country	2007 Research and Development Spending (Billions of Dollars)	Percent of 2007 Sales
Toyota	Japan	8.39	3.6
General Motors	USA	8.1	4.5
Ford	USA	7.5	4.3
Honda	Japan	5.14	4.9
Volkswagen	Europe	4.76	3.2
Daimler	Europe	4.32	3.2
Nissan	Japan	4	4.2
BMW	Europe	4	5.2
Peugeot	Europe	2.84	3.4
Denso Corp.	Japan	2.72	7.7

Source: Crain Communications. *Automotive News*, 27 October 2008, and Booz & Co. Global Innovation 1,000 report.

Table 2.12: R&D spending (US$ billion) in 2007 by automobile industry leaders.

Region	R&D Spending (US$ billion)
Asia	20.25
Europe	15.92
USA	15.6

objective is to use the campus in Shanghai to bring different R&D centres to one location to increase internal collaboration and efficiency. The second is to adopt an open innovation concept to collaborate with external parties by making the campus available for them to work with their scientists and engineers. Their targeted external partners are hail from universities and research institutes and other companies including their vendors.

Xerox established its Open Innovation R&D Hub in Chennai, India in March 2010.[30] One of the goals is to collaborate with more local companies, government agencies and industries (both existing and new start-ups) to co-invent with external partners. They came up with an interesting concept that for every researcher they hire, they will aim to partner with at least 50 or more external partners. Their strategy is to have every researcher work on at least five projects, with each project having at least ten external partners. The model of one internal researcher targeting at least 50 external scientists, engineers or researchers will have a tremendous multiplier effect in tapping the talent of Indian scientists and engineers from both universities and industries.

---

[30] Xerox launches Innovation Hub in India, http://news.xerox.com/pr/xerox/xerox-launches-India-innovation-hub-155321.aspx.

Innovative companies continue to invest in research and development with the strategic intention to build on their future, to take advantage of opportunities, to acquire competitive advantage, and to increase their speed in penetrating the market with their new products.

China has transited from a centrally planned innovation system towards a more market-oriented open innovation system.[31]

With better dissemination of findings through research and enterprising talent returning from Europe or the USA to China or India, the practice of open innovations by companies, research institutions and universities will in fact accelerate a great deal of innovations in the Asia Pacific region.

2.6 OPEN BUSINESS ENVIRONMENT

According to a recent report from the World Economic Forum (WEF), the top two trade-conducive economies in the world are in Asia — Singapore and Hong Kong. Singapore received top marks for its open market, highly efficient and transparent border administration, well-developed transportation system and communication infrastructure, and an open business environment.

Singapore

Singapore is home to 26,000 international enterprises. Nearly half of those are from the USA, Europe and Japan. The remaining half of the international enterprises are from China, India and ASEAN respectively. Singapore serves as a regional hub for thousands of multinational enterprises.

To fuel the continued growth of an open business environment, Singapore is going a step further by creating a market

---

[31] Liu, X., Lundin N., *Towards a Market-based Open Innovation System in China.*

place for ideas and innovations. Singapore established Biopolis for biomedical research and Fusionopolis for science and engineering research. These are huge complexes for scientific communities who come from all corners of the world.

With 185,806 square metres or two million square feet of built-up area, Biopolis houses about 4,000 scientists and researchers focusing on biomedical research (see Figure 2.17).

Fusionopolis is the focal point for the information, communications, media, physical sciences and engineering research community (see Figure 2.18).

Professor Paul Herrling, Head of Corporate Research Novartis, shared his reasons for setting up the Novartis Institute for Tropical Diseases, their latest biotech R&D operation, in Singapore, "There are a number of important aspects that we take into account before deciding where to locate an R&D institute. These include the availability of talent, research environment, proximity to patients and treating doctors, public support for the biomedical sciences, regulatory environment and good IP protection. Singapore meets all these criteria. It has also established an excellent scientific network and made the biomedical sciences one of its top priorities."

Figure 2.17: Biopolis for biomedical research.

Figure 2.18:   Fusionopolis for science & engineering research.

Singapore's vision of setting up a Campus for Research Excellence and Technological Enterprise (CREATE)[32] at the cost of S$360 million in 2009 is now in the final phase of implementation. The physical building was completed in July 2011. The current NRF office in the city centre will be relocated to CREATE Tower in September 2011. Towards the end of 2011, all CREATE centres currently housed in NUS or NTU will be relocated to the new premises.

CREATE will have top international researchers to work alongside Singapore-based collaborators. It is will serve as a forum for the exchange of new knowledge and ideas, cross-pollination of ideas and transformation of ideas to be implemented in the market

---

[32] Source: National Research Foundation, Singapore, http://www.nrf. gov.sg/nrf/uploadedFiles/Publications/CREATE%20Project%20Brief.pdf.

Figure 2.19: Campus for Research Excellence and Technological Enterprise (CREATE).

place for the benefit of society at large. The multi-cultural and multi-disciplinary community of 1,000 top researchers will interact and work together in this "research & technological eco-system and hub" that is also co-located within new NUS University Town of the National University of Singapore.

Singapore's vision of becoming a key enabler of Research and Innovation for the global community can be summarized in Dr Tony Tan's (Chairman of NRF in July 2009) comments at the launch of the construction of CREATE complex: "It (CREATE) will act as a magnet to attract scientific talent from around the globe". Please see: http://www.nrf.gov.sg/nrf/uploadedFiles/News_and_Events/Speeches/2009/OPENING%20REMARKS%20BY%20DR%20TONY%20TAN.pdf; http://newshub.nus.edu.sg/news/0907/PDF/RESEARCH-bt-29Jul-p2.pdf.

In the words of Mr. Teo Ming Kian, Permanent Secretary for National Research and Development, "CREATE would bring about a new paradigm of global collaboration in creating and multiplying intellectual capital. CREATE would be the home to research centres of world renowned institutions and a vibrant community — a place where researchers, scientists, academia, entrepreneurs, angel investors, venture capitalists, intellectual property experts and technology transfer professionals can gather to meet, be inspired, do research and bring ideas to the market for the benefits of economy and society". Please see: http://www.nrf. gov.sg/nrf/default.aspx?id=1814.

Singapore is now ranked number 1 in the Global Innovation Index (Boston Consulting Group) in the innovation list comprising of 110 countries. Please see: http://www.globalinnovationindex. org/gii/GII%20COMPLETE_PRINTWEB.pdf.

Corporate Tax Rate in Singapore for 2009 — Amongst the Most Competitive

Most Asian countries are making their corporate tax rates competitive to attract foreign direct investments. Singapore is no exception. Singapore continues to benchmark itself against the global corporate tax rate and adopts a business friendly approach to attract foreign direct investments. From a high corporate tax rate of 40 percent in 1986, this has been reduced to 17 percent in year 2011 (for income earned in 2010) (see Figure 2.20). This is comparable to Hong Kong's corporate tax rate of 16.5 percent. In addition, Singapore has zero tax for dividend and capital gain.

Ease of Doing Business

In a recent publication by the World Bank and the International Finance Corporation, "Doing Business 2009",[33] it is mentioned that "Singapore continues to rank at the top for

---

[33] Doing Business 2009, World Bank and International Finance Corporation, p. 3.

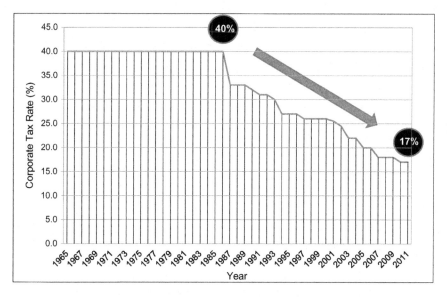

Figure 2.20: Making corporate tax rate attractive for investments in Singapore.

Source: IRAS, Singapore

the ease of doing business". Among the top 25 economies, 8 are from Asia Pacific (see Table 2.13). Asia Pacific countries with their open business environments and less hassles in conducting businesses will continue to fuel the shift of investments and innovation to Asia Pacific.

Singapore institutions have been benchmarking themselves against the global best for many years. External benchmarks propelled Singapore institutions into attaining world-class standards. Several Asian countries are following similar models to become world class-institutions.

The "doing business" ranking methodology is based upon the following factors:

1. Starting a business
2. Dealing with construction permits
3. Employing workers
4. Registering property

71

Table 2.13:   Ranking of ease of doing business.

Economy	Ranking in 2009	Ranking in 2008	Region
Singapore	1	1	Asia Pacific
New Zealand	2	2	Asia Pacific
United States	3	3	North America
Hong Kong, China	4	4	Asia Pacific
Denmark	5	5	Europe
United Kingdom	6	6	Europe
Ireland	7	7	Europe
Canada	8	8	North America
Australia	9	10	Asia Pacific
Norway	10	9	Europe
Iceland	11	11	Europe
Japan	12	12	Asia Pacific
Thailand	13	19	Asia Pacific
Finland	14	13	Europe
Georgia	15	21	Eastern Europe
Saudi Arabia	16	24	Middle East
Sweden	17	14	Europe
Bahrain	18	17	Middle East
Belgium	19	16	Europe
Malaysia	20	25	Asia Pacific
Switzerland	21	15	Europe
Estonia	22	18	Eastern Europe
South Korea	23	22	Asia Pacific
Mauritius	24	29	Africa
Germany	25	20	Europe

5. Getting credit
6. Protecting investors
7. Paying taxes
8. Trading across borders
9. Enforcing contracts
10. Closing a business

The two most populous nations in Asia Pacific — China and India — are making systematic regulatory reforms. In 2008, China ranked 151st and moved up to the 144th position in 2009. Over the past five years, the Chinese government has committed to a systematic regulatory reform and is making progress. One of the major reforms made was the major reduction in corporate tax rate from 33.3 percent to 25 percent. Another major progress made was in the area of protecting investors. India ranked 120th in 2008 and 122nd in 2009. India is undergoing systematic regulatory reform and has focused on using IT technology to implement the electronic registration of new businesses, electronic collateral registry and online submission of customs forms and payments.

Many Asian countries are also pursuing similar initiatives. In addition, Special Economic Zones (SEZs) are being created by South Korea, China and India to spur economic growth. These SEZs are export-oriented open business ecosystems. The SEZs are stepping stones to transit from an export-oriented economy to a market economy. The strategy is to build on the success of an export-oriented and market economy and then move towards developing technology-intensive industries. Currently, many SEZs are in the process of establishing research and innovation centers. One strategic thrust is to welcome multinational enterprises to set up R&D and innovation centres.

These systematic regulatory reforms that work towards a model of open business environment to attract multi-national enterprises to set up research and development centres in Asia Pacific will aid in sustaining and building the momentum of new knowledge creation and innovations in the Asia Pacific region.

2.7 TEST-BEDDING INNOVATIONS AND SETTING NEW BENCHMARKS

Asian countries have embarked on mega projects for the test-bedding of innovations and best practices. Some key examples in the following sections show such test-beds and innovations which are helping Asia Pacific economies to fare better.

Singapore Multi-Purpose Marina Barrage

Singapore is an island nation and a city with a population of about five million. With only 710 square kilometres of land, it has no natural resources and has to harness every drop of rainfall and find ways to reuse waste water.

The Singapore Marina Barrage is conceptualised to be a holistic approach to water management. Its water management project has three main purposes:

1. It acts as a tidal barrier to alleviate floods in low-lying areas.
2. It creates an additional source of water supply.
3. Its water features/facilities allow recreational use and serve as a lifestyle attraction.

The Singapore Marina Barrage is a 350 metre-long barrage (dam) built across the Marina Channel, the estuary of the Singapore river (see Figure 2.21). This barrage is used to create a fresh-water reservoir by separating the sea water, as well as to keep out the tide. One unique feature of this barrage is that the nine 30-metre steel crest gates are hydraulically operated to be raised or lowered depending on the weather or tide. If high tide coincides with heavy rainfall, there are seven 40 cubic metre per

Figure 2.21: The Singapore Marina Barrage spans the Marina Channel and allows visitors to walk across both the reservoir and sea.

second pumps to pump excess storm water from the reservoir. In this way, floods in low-lying areas of Singapore can be prevented.

The reservoir is developed for recreational activities such as windsurfing, waterfront dining, boating, and water sports. The barrage was built using eco-friendly technologies with an iconic green roof to act as an insulation layer to lower the temperature of the building below and to serve as a recreational field. A solar park of more than 400 solar panels was built nearby to supply energy for the building.

The futuristic Singapore Marina Barrage, with these innovative eco-friendly features, won the prestigious Green Award from the American Academy of Environmental Engineers in May 2009.

Singapore — Green Solutions

Singapore is also designing and developing smart grids for clean electricity generation and distribution. Such an example can be found on the island of Pulan Ubin (see Figure 2.22)

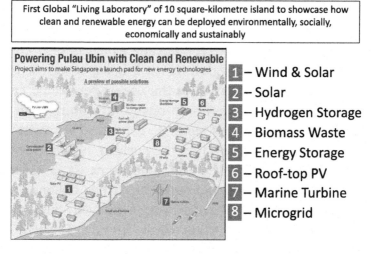

First Global "Living Laboratory" of 10 square-kilometre island to showcase how clean and renewable energy can be deployed environmentally, socially, economically and sustainably

Powering Pulau Ubin with Clean and Renewable
Project aims to make Singapore a launch pad for new energy technologies

1 – Wind & Solar
2 – Solar
3 – Hydrogen Storage
4 – Biomass Waste
5 – Energy Storage
6 – Roof-top PV
7 – Marine Turbine
8 – Microgrid

Figure 2.22: Singapore's Pulau Ubin is used for test-bedding of renewable energy.

Source: Energy Market Authority (EMA) Singapore

India — Solar Lanterns, Solar Cookers and Solar Water Heaters for the Rural Areas

Concentrated electrictiy generation and long distance transmission do not address the energy needs as Asia and Africa are home to millions of people who do not have grid electricity connections. According to one estimate, India alone has one hundred million people who rely on kerosene-wick lanterns for lighting. These lanterns emit poor light as well as harmful fumes. One kerosene lantern emits about one ton of carbon over a period of ten to fifteen years. Innovations harnessing breakthroughs in science and technologies, for example, solar photovoltaic technologies, are helping these disadvantaged people.

Solar lanterns, solar cookers, and solar water heaters are a few examples of innovations based on advanced solar photovoltaic concepts.

In addition, an Indian company, Vihaan Networks Limited (VNL), developed a solar-powered base station for cell phone networks. The cell phone base stations are powered by solar energy with a 72-hour battery backup which is also charged using solar energy. This innovation will bring benefits to the rural areas of India and promote the use of renewable energy. These VNL WorldGSM system-based stations need only between 50 W and 120 W of power to operate. This saves great amounts of energy compared to the current typical GSM station that requires 3000 W diesel generators. It is estimated that these generators are currently using two billion litres of diesel a year in India. This innovation by VNL made it the Bronze winner of The Asian Wall Street Journal 2009 Technology Innovation Awards (The Asian Wall Street Journal, 14 September 2009).

China Railway Systems

Qinghai-Tibet Railway Line

China undertook a massive and innovative high altitude rail project that crosses China from Qinghai to Tibet through landscapes ranging from grassland to permafrost. The Qinghai-Tibet railway line is the railway system with the highest altitude in the world, the highest point being 5,072 metres or 16,640 feet above sea level at Tanggula Pass (higher than Mt Blanc at 4,810 metres or 15,780 feet). This high-altitude railway runs a total length of 1,956 kilometres (1,213 miles) of which more than a quarter (about 550 kilometres or 342 miles) of the railway is on permafrost (see Figures 2.23 and 2.24).

The permafrost posed a major challenge to Chinese engineers. In summer, with the thawing of uppermost layer, the ground becomes muddy and the land can sink up to 15 metres.

Figure 2.23:   Section of the Qinghai-Tibet railway.

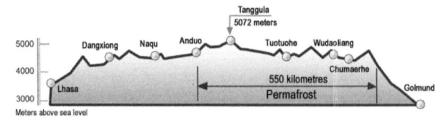

Figure 2.24: Vertical Sectional Diagram (Golmund–Lhasa section of Qinghai–Tibet Railway).

Chinese engineers used an innovative approach by building elevated tracks with foundations sunk deep into the ground. To keep the rail bed frozen, hollow concrete pipes were sunk beneath the tracks, and metal sun shades were used to shield the ice from strong sunlight. Key portions of the track are also passively cooled with ammonia-based heat exchangers.

This Qinghai and Tibet high altitude railway system will promote economic growth in this remote area.

China — High Speed Magnetic Levitation (Maglev) Rail System

China is prepared to test-bed a foreign high speed magnetic levitation (Maglev) system developed by Germany and use it commercially. The first Shanghai Maglev uses magnets to move the train up to a speed of 430 kilometres per hour (kph) or 270 miles per hour (mph) (see Figure 2.25). As it "floats" above the railway line, the noise level is rather low and it consumes much less energy than the traditional railway system. China first test-bedded this Maglev train system with a 30 kilometre-long line from Shanghai city, Longyang Road to Shanghai Pudong International Airport. This journey which normally would have taken 30 minutes by road, now takes only eight minutes.

With the experience gained from the Shanghai maglev project, China is moving on to intercity transportation. In 2010,

Figure 2.25: Shanghai Maglev train.

China will begin the construction of the next Maglev from Shanghai to Hangzhou, a 200 kilometres (124 miles) long Maglev train system. This maglev train will have a maximum speed of 450 kph. A one-way journey is expected to take 30 minutes as compared to the traditional train which takes up to two hours. China's test-bedding of transportation systems is setting new benchmarks for cleaner and more efficient mass movement of people between cities.

China — "New Silk Roads of Steel"

The Ministry of Railways in China is planning to extend its high speed rail network. This "new silk road of steel" rail system of 81,000 kilometres will connect to 28 countries. The master plan has three lines that will connect Asia and Europe by 2025. One line will start from western China, in the city of Kunming in Yunnan Province, and run southwards to end in Singapore. The second line will start in Urumqi in Xinjiang Province and connect Kazakhstan, Uzbekistan and Turkmenistan with Germany. The third line will start from northern China, in the city of Heilongjiang via Russia to eastern and southern Europe.

These "new silk roads of steel" will enable China to have easy access to natural resources like oil and gas from Myanmar, Iran and Russia.

Thus over a short period of six years (from 2004 when China acquired high-speed rail technology from France, Japan, Canada and Germany) China developed high-speed rail systems that can reach a speed of over 350 kph to undertake the massive 25-year "New Silk Roads of Steel" project.

China — Green Initiatives

China recognises that its expanding industrial activities and urbanisation are leading to the emission of large quantities of greenhouse gases. In order to mitigate this situation, China has invested in clean energy generation projects and the building of eco-friendly cities. According to the United Nations Environment Program report, China invested slightly more than US$ 15 billion in green projects in 2008. This amounted to about 10 percent of global spending (US$ 155 billion) in sustainable energy investments worldwide.

China's policy makers are embracing green technology as a driver of economic growth and are stepping up their efforts on energy conservation, greenhouse gas emission reduction and environmental protection projects.

Social Innovation

With the growing trend of philanthropists contributing towards social enterprises, Singapore's philanthropic foundation, the Lien Foundation[34] (http://www.lienfoundation.org/),

---

[34] Radical Philanthropy: The Lien Foundation takes a radical approach and invest in innovative solutions that often challenge existing conventions.

test-bedded in collaboration with the Singapore Management University to work on a project to promote social innovation. This social innovation project, called the LIEN i3 Challenge, was launched in January 2009 in Singapore. The aim was to catalyse social projects that are innovative, implementable and impactful (3I's) in Singapore and Asia. It tapped global talent by

Table 2.14: Winners of Lien 3 challenge that involved science & technology.

Winner	Country/Countries of Collaboration	Winning Innovative Projects
1	Tanzania–Thailand	HeroRats — Rats to identify and locate landmines more quickly and more safely than humans
2	Singapore — Batam, Indonesia	Interlocking Brick — An alternative brick research and production centre to provide eco-friendly and cost-saving homes for Indonesian villagers
3	Singapore	Intelligent Walking Aid — To create a navigation aid using RFID and mobile technologies so that the visually handicapped can "see" and hear their way around the Housing Development Board (HDB) Hub
4	Sri Lanka	Shilpa Sayura e-School — To leverage on an existing IT infrastructure to provide Sri Lankan villagers with an alternative teaching platform that promotes self-learning
5	Switzerland–Cambodia	To construct a steam pump in a sustainable model that provides a cost-effective irrigation solution to remote villages and farming communities in Cambodia with no carbon footprint

encouraging all nationals (either as individuals or as a group) to contribute ideas.

In just three months, a total of 648 entries around the world were received. This avalanche of applications was unexpected, but it demonstrated clearly that the globalisation or internationalisation of a social project has a distinct benefit.

From those 648 entries, eight winners were selected. The winning entries reflected the innovative ideas from members of the global community who are passionate to contribute towards the betterment of society without being driven by the profit motive (see Table 2.14).

Test-bedding of new social innovations is catching on. Governments in Asia are encouraging successful enterpreneurs to contribute back to the society. This new group of philantheropists are trying new ways to contribute to society.

One of the key factors for a successful Global Research Foundation initiative will be to tap on this new pool of philanthropists and new philanthropy foundations set up by these new groups of successful entrepreneurs that have benefited from the rapid economic growth in Asia.

Chapter 3

INFLUENCERS

For the first time in history, more than half the world consists of middle-class people. More than half of the world's population is living in urban cities. We are one of the few generations who will see the doubling of the population in our lifetime.

The changing demography poses several challenges and opportunities. Mankind will be challenged to find more innovative and novel ways to house and feed people and provide enough clean water, energy and healthcare for them. In addition, global climate changes, a rapidly ageing population, and the spread of infectious and emerging diseases will continue to be mankind's greatest challenges.

Globalisation and increased connectivity around the world are great opportunities for the research community, governments and industries to rise to the challenge and be prepared for the future.

3.1 POPULATION GROWTH

The global demographic landscape is changing rapidly. Population dynamics influence every aspect of human, ecological, social, economic development and the drive for innovations. Innovations in turn have helped to accommodate the increase in population and improve the earth's capacity to carry the increased population.

Medical science discoveries have reduced infant deaths and increased life expectancies. Innovations in sanitation and water management have reduced many water-borne diseases that kill people.

Science and engineering discoveries and innovations have changed the way we travel. Our parents took a month to travel via the "slow boat" from China or India in the mid 1990s. Today, air travel from the southern part of China to the southern part of India only takes five hours of flight. The increased mobility of people and talent is causing many of them to move to urban cities in search of better opportunities and quality of life.

The new demographic landscape with higher mobility of talent provides opportunities for scientists and researchers to collaborate on research projects that focus on finding sustainable solutions that will benefit mankind.

Figure 3.1 shows global population growth for the past two thousand years, and projects population growth up to 2050.

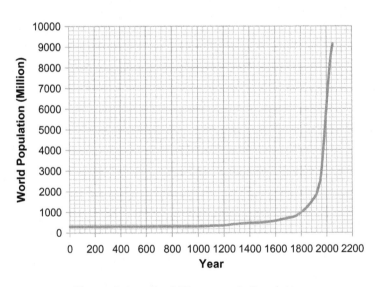

Figure 3.1:   Rapid Increase in Population

Source: http://www.census.gov/ipc/www/worldhis.html

RAPID INCREASE IN POPULATION

The earth's population first reached one billion in 1804. In 2009, 205 years later, the population had increased by more than six times to 6.8 billion people.

It is projected that the population will reach eight billion in 2025 and nine billion in 2054. Table 3.1 shows the time intervals between every one billion increase in the world population. It took 1804 years to reach the one billion mark and only 123 years after that to reach the two billion mark. Thereafter, each additional one billion jump in the world's population only required an interval of less than 100 years.

From a Young World to an "Older" World

The growing population began with a "young world", where the majority of the people were young people with increasing life expectancy, but we are seeing a higher proportion of senior people above the age of 65. It is projected that by 2050, one

Table 3.1: Rapid population growth — shorter time intervals for each one billion increase in population.

Year	World Population	Interval in Years
950	250 million	
1600	500 million	650
1804	1 billion	204
1927	2 billion	123
1960	3 billion	33
1974	4 billion	14
1987	5 billion	13
1999	6 billion	12
2013	7 billion	14
2025	8 billion	12
2054	9 billion	29

Source: United Nations.

in every six people will be above 65 years old. This rapid demographic shift to an ageing population is largely due to an increase in life expectancy and declines in infant mortality and birth rates. It is projected that by the year 2050, there will be two billion people over the age of 60. With this shift, there are going be social-economic challenges in the long term. One key challenge will be to provide sufficient healthcare services for this "silver generation".

Increasing Life Expectancy

Shifting Population Trend

Population growth and global mobility of talent will play an influential role in shaping the nature of politics, economics and innovation internationally over the next few decades. The bulk of the world's population is now in Asia Pacific.

There are four key trends in the migration of talent. First, the bulk of migration will be intra-country from rural to urban cities, especially in the two large Asian countries: China and India. The second will be the flow of talent internationally among developing countries. The third will be the flow of talent from developing to developed countries. The fourth will be the "Intellectual Diaspora" — the scientists and scholars from India and China who left their countries from the 1960s onwards to study in the USA or Europe, and who are now returning to their home countries.

With availability and mobility of skilled and technically talented people, major city centres in Asia will be able to penetrate markets in a shorter time with their new innovations. This in turn will drive the establishment of more global headquarters and research and development centres in Asia Pacific by major multi-national enterprises. An example of this shift is the setting up of Caltex's global headquarters in Singapore in 1999.

Caltex moved its operating headquarters to Singapore from the USA and shifted operations from a geographic to a functional organisation in order to meet the challenges of the 21st century. Caltex was the first Fortune 500 Company to receive Global Headquarters status from Singapore's Economic Development Board.[35]

China and India have become preferred destinations for research and development centres of major multi-national enterprises. It is estimated that by the end of 2008, multi-national enterprises will have established over 1,000 research and development centres in China alone.

The new demography and higher population growth in developing countries will result in new challenges in providing food. On the brighter side, the growing population provides the opportunity to tap this growing pool of young talent.

3.2 ECONOMIC GROWTH

With increased investments in innovations that are supported by academia, businesses, government and non-governmental agencies, we can observe that economic growth has local, regional and global impacts. We have seen that global investment in research and development has been increasing, and Asia Pacific countries' rate of increase in research and development has accelerated more than that of Europe and the USA.

Figure 3.2 illustrates that untill the Industrial Revolution, Asia Pacific economics represented about half of the world's GDP. We can see the evolution of the world economy has involved innovation from the ancient, classical and modern eras. The Silk Roads from China to Central Asia, India and Europe created a new transcontinental system of trade. Marco Polo

---

[35] Source: www.caltex.com, Caltex in Singapore.

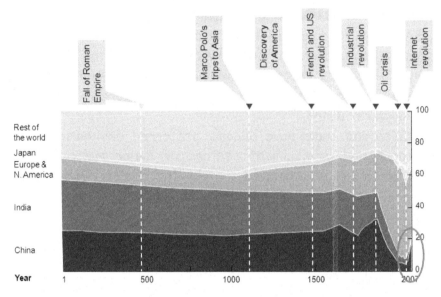

Figure 3.2:   Share of total world GDP (1 AD–2007 AD), GDP share in percentage. Asia's GDP was more than half of the world's GDP.

Source: Angus Madison's "Historical Statistics for the World Economy: 1-2004 AD", Deutsche Bank Global Market Research.

was able to take the Silk Road from Europe to Asia and trade in Chinese-made silk, spices and precious metals. After the Industrial Revolution which began in 1700 in the UK and spread quickly to Europe and then to the USA, the world economy was dominated by Europe and America. The turning point came in the year 2008 when Asia Pacific represented half of the world's economy again.

In Figures 2.1 and 3.4, we see the increased research funding in Asia Pacific countries, indicating a positive correlation between economic growth and investment in innovations.

The current shift in relative wealth and economic power from the Atlantic to the Pacific (especially China and India) will also encourage more investment in innovations in Asia Pacific.

In the year 1600, the GDP per capita was $596. By year 2000, it had grown ten times to $6,055 (See Figure 3.3).

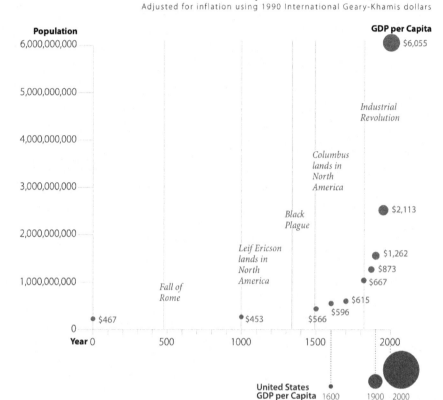

World Income and Population for last 2,000 Years
Adjusted for inflation using 1990 International Geary-Khamis dollars

Figure 3.3: World income and population for the last 2,000 years.

Going by GDP (PPP), Asia is home to the 2nd (China), 3rd (Japan) and 4th (India) largest economies in the world.

In terms of it is predicted that Asia will garner half of the global GDP share. Asia is set to become an economic centre of power and influence in the 21st century.

The continued global economic growth plus the addition of 1.2 billion people by 2025 will put tremendous pressure on energy, food and water resources. With the ease of migration,

89

globalisation and speedy information flows brought about by improved ICT, it will be difficult for individual nations to address all these societal challenges alone. We need a global community which has more resources and that is better equipped to tackle these issues. This will drive governments to put aside resources to find innovative solutions.

China and India

Two centuries ago, China produced about 30 percent and India about 15 percent of global wealth. Today, the economic power-houses of China and India are once again restoring the position of Asia's global wealth to the same levels that they were at two centuries ago.

China

Foreign reserves topped $1 trillion in late 2006 and $2 trillion in April 2009. China's holdings of USA Treasury Bills is expected to top $1 trillion in 2012.

India

India has experienced a transition from prosperity to poverty and back to prosperity again. India was once a premier economic power. Its wealth in the period between 1500 to 1700 was about a quarter of the world's economy. Its share started to decline after the early 19th century, gradually at first, then precipitously. In 1950, just three years after India emerged as an independent nation, its share of the global GDP was down to a mere 4.17 percent. It was only in the 1990s that India, for the first time in 300 years, saw its share of the world output increasing (see Table 3.2). The country is on its journey back to prosperity.

Table 3.2: India's share of the world economy.

India's Share of World Economy (percent)

Year	1500	1600	1700	1820	1900	1950	1990	2000
Share	24.36	22.43	24.44	16.02	8.6	4.17	4.05	5.27

Source: Angus Maddison.

Table 3.3: USA trade balance of high-technology manufactured goods.

USA Trade balance of high-technology manufactured products

Year	US$ Billion
1990	+54
2001	−50

Shift of Trade in High-Technology Manufactured Products

In 1990, the trade balance of high-technology products was more than US$54 billion.

As shown in Table 3.3, in 2001, the trade balance of high-technology products was negative.

In a decade, the USA trade balance of high-technology products showed a negative value.

Challenges and Opportunities Under the Current Economic Situation

New knowledge and innovations can be key factors that spur economic recovery.

During the financial crisis of 1977, South Korea suffered badly. Since then, South Korea has undergone a metamorphosis, with information and communication technologies (ICT) and innovation becoming the power engines for its recovery and enviable economic growth.

The Korean government encouraged Korean corporations and universities to speed up innovations in seven key sectors: the internet, broadband convergence, mobile communication services, commerce, dissemination of financial information and the IT industry.

Today, Korea is ranked 1st and 3rd in terms of the broadband internet penetration rate and internet usage ratio respectively. The IT industry has grown drastically by an annual rate that has averaged 18.8 percent since 1998, and has become the growth engine for the country's economic evolution. By the end of 2003, the Korean IT industry represented 15.6 percent of GDP and 30 percent of the country's exports.

To build on this momentum, Korea developed "the road to $20,000 GDP/capita — IT839" strategy in 2004. The purpose of this strategy is to help Korea stay ahead of the global competition by being innovative.

Korea's government initiatives in setting up techno-parks, technology innovation centres and technology business incubators have helped start-up ventures and entrepreneurs a great deal. There are many regional research centres that support existing technological research centres at the university level that in turn give local industries an impetus by providing manpower and a knowledge base.

Korea today is one of the most inventive nations in the world. It is now ranked 7th in the number of utility patents in the Global Competitive Report.

3.3 URBANISATION

Urbanisation can be defined as the shift from a rural to an urban society. More than half of the world's population has been living in urban cities (see Figure 3.4). The rapidity of

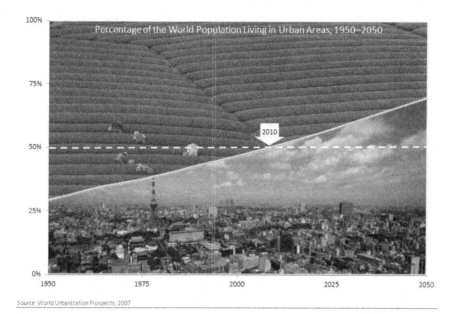

Source: World Urbanization Prospects, 2007

Figure 3.4: Half of the world's population is living in urban cities.

urbanisation is greatest in Africa and Asia. As the income gap between urban and rural societies continues to widen, the migration of people from the rural areas to the cities to seek better opportunities is unstoppable.

While increased urbanisation may have some positive impacts such as lower birth rate due to city lifestyle as well as better access to cultural and educational opportunities, scientists are becoming more concerned about the issues regarding the sustainability of resources and the environment.

Rapid urbanisation poses challenges for housing, transportation, energy, water, healthcare, sanitation and sewage disposal.

Historically, urbanisation is closely associated with industrialisation. Cities are ideal places to have factories and hire workers. In addition, cities are also closely associated with the research and development centres of universities, industries and governmental agencies. Therefore, as more cities are formed and more cities transform into mega-cities, more research and development centres will be set up, especially in Asia.

Universities, research centres of industries and research institutions of government agencies are interacting more closely and synergistically to create a new knowledge base for their cities and regions as they have realised that understanding the local and regional differences are of critical importance for urban economic growth and change.

With the mobility of the international talent pool of scientists and engineers, lower startup and operational costs of research and development centres, good governmental support in the form of tax incentives and almost universal access to information via the internet, Asia will have more and more creative knowledge clusters. With an increased understanding of its own local and regional needs, Asia is well placed to meet the challenges of rapid urbanisation unique to each country and region, and is beginning to bring this new confidence to undertake mega and inter-country projects with innovative solutions to tackle issues associated with urbanisation and create models that are scalable and transferrable to other countries.

Political leaders in Asia are prepared to collaborate on innovative and mega projects that draw upon science and technology experts to provide novel and innovative solutions. Together with investments from global industries and inter-government, they aim to make new models of liveable and sustainable cities.

A recent Asian example is the Sino–Tianjin eco-city development project.

In 2007, China and Singapore embarked on a joint eco city project: the Sino–Tianjin eco-city development. This eco-city project entailed the conversion of a 30 square-kilometre piece of land that is currently uninhabitable to an eco-friendly city with a budget of 50 billion Yuan (estimated US$7.3 billion) within 10 to 15 years for a population of 350,000, is truly ambitious and mind-boggling. To fulfil this vision, the best minds, latest science and engineering technologies will be needed.

Asian leaders understand that to provide for the future needs and aspiration of the people, more new cities will be needed. New models of liveable and sustainable cities will be needed in the Asia Pacific region. This new model will use "green technologies" and urban "eco" strategies to combat and mitigate climate change with the understanding that there is a limit to earth's carrying capacity.

The eco-city project is located 40 kilometres from Tianjin city and 150 kilometres from Beijing, the capital city of China. This piece of land was chosen as it has the most unfavurable features that a normal developer will not even contemplate. The soil has high salinity and the area lacks water resources.

Innovative green technologies incorporate the recycling of refuse, sewage and waste water, and the buildings will be energy efficient. 90 percent of the residents will also be making "green trips" by walking, cycling or using public transport to reduce carbon emissions.

The urban "eco" planning will incorporate concepts of eco-economy, eco-residence, eco-culture, a harmonious community and scientific management.

A master plan for this eco-city project will be used as a model for the building of future cities to address the issues of climate change and the challenge of harmonising rapid economic growth with sustainable development for a better quality of life for all.

In the 1980s, the urban population accounted for only 20 percent of China's population. According to the latest Blue Book of Cities in China, published by the Chinese Academy of Social Sciences, (CASS), nearly 50 percent of China's population now live in urban areas, which is more than 600 million people.

Table 3.4: World capitals of the future.[36]

Forbes list of World Capitals of the Future		Current Leading Global Centres	
Capital	Country	Capital	Country
Shanghai and Beijing	China	Tokyo	Japan
Moscow	Russia	London	United Kingdom
Mumbai	India	Paris	France
Sao Paulo	Brazil	New York, Chicago, Los Angeles	United States
Dubai	United Arab Emirates	Seoul	South Korea
Calgary	Canada	Singapore	Singapore
Perth	Australia	Hong Kong	Greater China
Houston and Dallas	United States		

As more and more cities and mega-cities are formed in Asia, particularly in China and India, there will be more new centres of knowledge creation and discovery.

Over a short period of 25 years, the per capita income based on Purchasing Power Parity (PPP) grew by 1,500 percent for China, 400 percent for India and 245 percent for the USA The rapid urbanisation of cities with their modern amenities and new lifestyles made them attractive places for many of the scholars and academicians who left their countries.

---

[36] Source: Forbes — World Capitals of the Future.

With a strong manufacturing base, the capitals of the future are attracting more and more R&D centres to be set up near production facilities.

These new world capitals in turn become new knowledge and innovation centres, which will be the catalysts to sustain the new knowledge-intensive economy of the world.

However, there is much more that can be done to mitigate the issues of sustainability of rapid urbanisation.

Urban solutions are needed for urban mobility, urban agriculture, water and energy, environment diversity, security and safety, information and communication technologies, health and cultural developments for harmonious living.

All these will influence the quality and sustainability of future mankind.

3.4 INFORMATION AND COMMUNICATION TECHNOLOGY (ICT)

The first revolution of information and knowledge transfer started with the invention of written languages and it was enhanced by the invention of paper in Asia. It became the first platform to transfer knowledge across borders. The spread of knowledge was dependent on physical travel distances and the number of handwritten copies.

The second revolution was the development of movable-type system of printing in China, Korea and the invention of the printing press in Germany that led to the printing of books. With the ability to quickly produce multiple copies, these inventions allowed information reach a greater number of people. This was still very dependent on physical books and face to face contacts.

The third revolution was the internet and digitisation of information and knowledge. This third revolution transformed the dissemination information and knowledge.

With the combination of satellite television, radio, the internet, computers, telecommunications, mobile phones and emails for communications, the convergence of information and communication technologies make the world a "global village". The digital global village is one huge system of interconnected networks that are interdependent on one another to function smoothly. Nations, economies, markets and supply chains are now interconnected all the time. All these constitute a wonderful platform for global collaboration. The investment in and building of the ICT infrastructure will make a great difference in influencing the speed and productivity of major innovation efforts throughout the world and reap the social and economic benefits of a knowledge economy.

The next challenge of ICT is to reach out to people who may not be literate enough to read and write. Voice recognition technology will be the next new wave that will enable such people to access the internet and the plethora of available information and technology to lift them out of the poverty cycle.

Open sources will also allow more people to gain access to ICT without the need to tackle IP and licensing issues.

The common economic factors of production are land, labour and capital. In the new "e-world", land and labour take on a new dimension. The "land" of the cyber-world is borderless. An application made in Singapore for an office to be set in the country can be accessed across all countries without having to involve any physical movement of goods. This economic transaction of "knowledge" is has become a significant feature of the world economy. Microsoft and Google are examples of the changing landscape of the world economy due to ICT. The old economy was largely dependent on the size of land, labour and capital. Often, the extent of their endowment determined a nation's competitiveness and innovation capacity. The new e-economy is much more dependent on the connectedness of nations in the global economy. To make the quantum leap to join the global economy and make major contributions to the world economy, Asia Pacific countries made massive investments in setting up ICT infrastructures so as to increase their innovative capacity and competitiveness.

The connectedness will influence collaborations regionally and globally. There will be more opportunities for researchers to collaborate and hire talents around the world to solve societal challenges. Firms are also using ICT to develop new economic models such as the outsourcing of major call centres to countries like India and the Philippines.

The convergence of information and communication technologies (ICT) is a major influence of globalisation in the world. Information and communication technologies have dramatically changed the landscape of how people disseminate and communicate information and new knowledge. For many centuries, information was available in printed format; today, more and more information is available in digitised format. This digitised information and knowledge is available anytime and anywhere for anyone with computer and internet access. The ability to contribute and use information and knowledge simultaneously and communicate interactively has catalysed the rapid growth of a knowledge economy in the 21st century.

Today, we live in a new information age defined by connections. With the advancement of information and communication technology and increasing accessibility to the internet, the possibility for multi-party communication and interaction has increased. The world is experiencing a third revolution in the dissemination of knowledge through innovations in ICT.

All the major regions of the world have experienced more than doubling of the growth of internet users. The highest growth in the number of internet users over the nine years from 2000 was in Asia, which registered a growth of 518 percent (see Table 3.5).

Using data from December 2000 to June 2009, we see an increase in internet users by region from another perspective.

Table 3.5: Growth of internet users in the major regions of the world between December 2000 and June 2009.

Region	Dec 2000 No. of Internet Users	Jun 2009 No. of Internet Users	% Growth
Asia	114 million	704 million	518%
Europe	105 million	402 million	283%
North America	108 million	252 million	133%

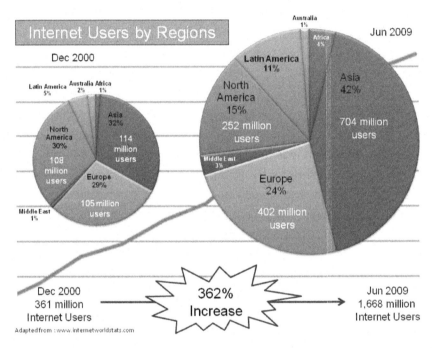

Figure 3.5: Exponential growth of internet users by regions from December 2000 to June 2009.[37]

The number of internet users in each region has increased, while the "pie" itself is getting bigger.

From December 2000 to June 2009, the increase in total number of internet users was 362 percent (see Figure 3.5).

---

[37] Source: http://www.internetworldstats.com/stats.htm.

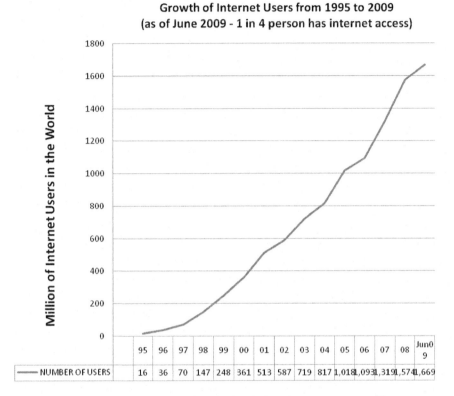

Growth of Internet Users from 1995 to 2009
(as of June 2009 - 1 in 4 person has internet access)

	95	96	97	98	99	00	01	02	03	04	05	06	07	08	Jun09
NUMBER OF USERS	16	36	70	147	248	361	513	587	719	817	1,018	1,093	1,319	1,574	1,669

Figure 3.6: Historical growth of global internet users.[38]

The growth of internet users would be more spectacular when we track it from 1995 to June 2009. There was a 10,331 percent increase in number of internet users from 16 million in 1995 to 1.6 billion in June 2009! (see Figure 3.6).

The scale of internet access and advancement in ICTs will provide the "speed to market" platform for researchers to translate their research into tangible products and services that meet the needs of society.

The "Internet Super Highway" enables researchers, business people, policy makers and consumers to debate on ideas,

---

[38] Source: www.internetworldstats.com.

share knowledge, expertise, and services interactively around the world at all times. This interactive cyber world has helped create and sustain opportunities for global and trans-border collaborations for scientific, social and economic developments on an unprecedented scale.

It is estimated that it will take 75 years for the telephone to reach 50 million users. The time for computers and television to do the same will take less than 20 years. For the internet to reach 50 million users, it may take only five years (see Figure 3.7). The capacity of mankind to adopt new useful technologies laid the ground work for global communications and the dissemination of information and knowledge. With the and ease in exchange of new ideas, more innovations will be spurred along the way.

As of June 2009, more than 1.6 billion people around the world were connected to the internet. The increase in internet access among the global population has been remarkable. In 1995, one in 25 people had internet access. Fourteen years later, one in every four people has internet access (see Table 3.6).

Although Asia has the most number of internet users in the world, the penetration of the population is the second lowest.

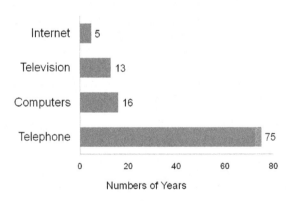

Figure 3.7: Number of years to reach 50 million users for key ICT technologies.

Table 3.6: Internet penetration as a percentage of population in June 2009.

Region	% Penetration as % of Population	Number of Internet Users (millions)	% of Internet Users in the world
Africa	6.7	66	4
Asia	18.5	704	42
Middle East	23.7	48	3
Latin America	30.0	176	11
Europe	50.1	402	24
Austrila	60.1	21	1
North America	73.9	252	15
World Average	24.7	1,669	100

Source: Internet World Stats — www.internetworldstats.com (June 2009 Figures).
Note: World Average Penetration Rate of 24.7% meant that on the average, 1 in every 4 people had internet access.

The potential of the internet in being the "broker of knowledge" in Asia will be unimaginable when the penetration reaches the same magnitude as that of the USA at 73.9 percent!

Nevertheless, in terms of the number of internet users, the Asia Pacific region has the highest number of internet users.

The World Wide Web has become the "global community" and the source of information and knowledge for the 1.6 billion global users, of which 704 million internet users (42 percent) are from Asia.

China has the highest number of internet users at 338 million (as of June 2009) in Asia (see Figure 3.8). This represents 20 percent of global internet users and 48 percent of Asia's internet users. Japan is the second followed by India in third position in terms of the number of internet users.

In Figure 3.8, we see China having the largest number of internet users at 338 million. The number of internet users in China is more than those in North America — 252 million internet users. With China's internet penetration rate of 25.3 percent, it has a potential for huge growth.

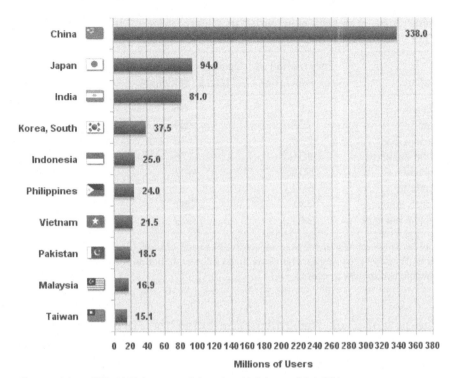

Source: Internet World Stats - www.internetworldstats.com/stats3.htm
Estimated Asia Internet users 704,213,930 for 2009 Q2
Copyright © 2009, Miniwatts Marketing Group

Figure 3.8: Top ten countries that have the highest number of internet users in Asia as of June 2009.[39]

In Figure 3.9, we see six countries in Asia Pacific with more than two-thirds of the population using the internet: South Korea, Japan, Hong Kong, Singapore, Taiwan and Malaysia. With high penetration rates of internet users in these Asia Pacific countries, open access to information and knowledge will enable these countries to communicate within their own regions and with the rest of the world. Researchers in these countries can

---

[39] Source: http://www.internetworldstats.com/stats3.htm.

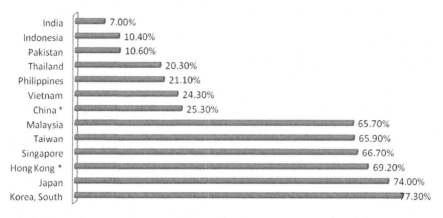

Figure 3.9: Penetration of internet users in Asia.

leverage on these platforms for broad surveys to test-bed their ideas and receive feedback. Government agencies in countries such as Japan, Korea and Singapore are using the internet for "e-governance", where payments for taxes, business registrations and transactions can be conducted. Governments in these countries are also using this "e-service" platform to receive feedback on their policies, including research initiatives.

Researchers and industries are also utilising the internet to host communication modes for their research.

The sheer number of people in Asia who have embraced this internet and digital platform or ICTs will bring more new innovations into the market place.

Innovations are going in full circle. And there is also a shift of ICT to Asia.

Asia's focus to leverage on IT to jump into the knowledge economy is very apparent. One key sign of this shift is that 50 percent of the current USA IT patents are from countries other than the USA.

The shift of ICT innovations to Asia Pacific is very apparent from the above analysis.

The next revolution will see the convergence of innovations where information and knowledge can be made more affordable and available anytime and anywhere.

This in turn will spur more innovations towards the solving the global challenges of population, economy, climate change, clean water, sustainable energy, rapid urbanisation, ageing, infectious and chronic diseases, food supplies and nutrition, and cyber security.

The internet and World Wide Web that started the Information Age will facilitate the 21st century renaissance. It may well speed up new inventions and innovation with a global community of researchers being able to connect interactively.

Sir Arthur C. Clarke, the author of the famous book, "*2001 — The Space Odyssey*", commented about the use of such information technologies:

> "…We now have to apply these technologies for saving lives, improving livelihoods and lifting millions of people out of squalor, misery and suffering…"

3.5 WATER

Here are some facts about water on earth:

- 75 percent of the earth is covered with water.
- 3 percent of the water is fresh water and the rest is saline water.
- Of all the fresh water on earth, less than 1 percent is accessible for direct human consumption.

Although there is "water water everywhere", not all water in the world is equally accessible or available. Today, more than

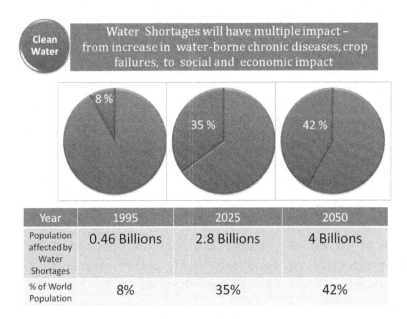

Year	1995	2025	2050
Population affected by Water Shortages	0.46 Billions	2.8 Billions	4 Billions
% of World Population	8%	35%	42%

Figure 3.10: Water shortages will increase and more people will be affected.

one billion members of the population are unable to have safe drinking water. This represents about 16 percent of the world's population.

With the current trend, it is projected that the shortage of water will worsen and have a greater impact on a global scale (see Figure 3.10).

Meeting the increasing demand for clean water is a global challenge. Population growth, rapid urbanisation, changing lifestyles, economic development and global climate change have led to increasing pressure on water resources everywhere. Polluted water from industries and agriculture is also linked to the spread of water-borne diseases and poisoning due to toxic chemicals and eutrophications.

Meteorological records and climate projections point to the fact that freshwater resources will be more scarce as a result of recent extreme weather patterns such as droughts and storms. The increase in variability and changes in water quantity and quality due to extreme weather patterns in several geographical areas will affect food supply and its availability.

Water scarcity is going to have three major influences in the 21st century:

1. Food security;
2. Health of aquatic ecosystems; and
3. Social and political instability.

Many of us do not realise that agricultural activities for the production of food are highly water-intensive. About two-thirds of all the water that we take from rivers, streams, lakes, and underground aquifers goes to agricultural activities of growing crops and raising animals for food. It is estimated that for every one ton of grains produced, about 1,000 tons of water will be needed. Over the next 30 years, with the increase in population that is projected to add another 2.6 billion people to the planet, it will be a huge challenge to source water for people to drink and grow food crops.

Singapore's Innovative Solution to the Water Resource Challenge

Forty years ago, Singapore had to ration water to conserve its scarce water resources. In addition to the limited water resources that Singapore faces today, there are also other challenges such as a growing population, economic development and changing lifestyles. To address the issue of water scarcity, Singapore adopted a technology and water resource management strategy called the "Four National Taps".

The "Four National Taps" strategy is based on four different sources of water supply:

1. Water from local catchments or reservoirs
2. Imported treated water from Malaysia
3. Reclaimed/recycled water from local waste water (branded NEWater)
4. Desalinated sea water

The first "tap" is the indigenous collection of rain water that flows into the local water catchments and reservoirs. Barrages or dams were built at several river mouths to increase the water catchment area. Pig farms were closed and relocated to neighbouring islands. All household waste water is piped to centralised waste water treatment plants. All industries pre-treat their waste water before transferring them through pipes to centralised waste water treatment plants. All storm water is channeled into local catchment areas.

The second "tap" refers to the imports of water from Malaysia. Treated water is brought to Singapore via the Johore/Singapore causeway. This is stored in the network of covered reservoirs.

The third "tap", NEWater, is recycled and treated effluent water from centralised water treatment plants that uses the latest recycling water technologies. The custom-built water recycling plant uses a three-stage process of ultra-filtration/microfiltration, reverse osmosis and ultraviolet radiation to reclaim water from the treated effluent water. Central to this is the 48 kilometre-long Deep Tunnel Sewerage System DTSS below the ground, which collects all the effluent water for recycling. The huge pipe (with a diameter that varies from 3.3 metres to 6.0 metres) network lies 23 metres to 39 meters below the ground. The principle of gravity flow effluent

Figure 3.11:   The Singapore Changi Water Reclamation Plant.

collection system eliminated the need for high energy consumption pumps and intermediate water collection centres. The DTSS pipes are sloped to reach the two centralised Water Reclamation Plants in the eastern and western parts of Singapore.

The Changi Water Reclamation Plant is located in the eastern part of Singapore. This DTSS was built at the cost of about S$2.2 billion over seven years. The current treatment capacity is 176 million gallons per day or 800,000 cubic metres per day. The ultimate future capacity will be 528 million gallons per day or 2,400,000 cubic metres per day.

The bold and innovative DTSS received worldwide recognition and was garnered the "Water Project of the Year" award at the Global Water Awards 2009.

The fourth "tap" is desalinated water obtained using reverse osmosis technology.

The "Four National Taps" is Singapore's strategic approach in using technology and sustainable water management principles to ensure that Singapore has a sufficient water supply to meet the needs of the growing population for the next 100 years.

We can develop new technologies to meet the challenges of water shortage. Time, leadership and funding will often be issues that are crucial in tackling these challenges. We believe that the water scarcity challenge is solvable.

We saw how Singapore can bring resources, technology and policies together that involve universities, private and public sectors to solve their water scarcity issue. We are sure that global collaborations can achieve even more.

3.6 ENERGY

When we talk about energy used in ancient times, we generally think of the muscle power in humans or domesticated animals such as buffaloes, bulls, donkeys and horses.

Today, we speak of energy as electrical power used for electricity generation, transportation and industries. With concerns about the Earth's carrying capacity for mankind, we now add on several dimensions when we discuss energy.

Energy, economy, population, environment and security are different dimensions but closely interlinked. The world is facing the challenge of securing affordable energy to fuel economic growth and satisfy the energy needs of the growing population. At the same time, the world needs to manage the associated environmental consequences and potential terrorism threat that may sabotage energy systems.

The diversification of the national energy mix is a cornerstone of every country that seeks energy security. In the wake of increasing demand for electricity, economic and population growth, and the pressing need to mitigate climate change and to ensure sustainable development, the global community is looking for energy innovations that are cost-effective, safe, environmentally sustainable and socially acceptable. The world desperately needs new energy technologies that are transformational. Global challenges need to be addressed by global solutions.

Despite all the efforts to find and use new sources of energy, the world today is still highly dependent on carbon-based fossil energy supply, as illustrated in the next five diagrams.

In 1973, 87 percent of the world energy supply was carbon-based fossil fuel. Thirty four years later, in 2007, 81 percent of the world energy supply was carbon-based fossil fuel. The world has made improvement towards less carbon-based fossil energy by 6 percent, but the world energy supply is still dependent mainly on carbon-based fossil energy. However, there are encouraging developments on the increase in the amount or quantity of renewables.

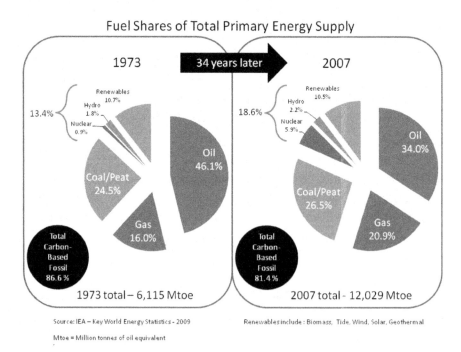

Figure 3.12: Shares of total primary energy supply by fuel type for 1973 and 2007 respectively.

Table 3.7: The total primary energy supply by fuel type — quantity and percentage increase over 34 years from 1973 to 2007.

Total Primary Energy Supply by Fuel			
	1973 (Mtoe)	2007 (Mtoe)	% Increase
Oil	2,819	4,090	45
Gas	978	2,514	157
Coal/Peat	1,498	3,188	113
Nuclear	55	710	1,190
Hydro	110	265	140
Renewables	654	1,263	93
Total	6,115	12,029	97

Mtoe = Million tonnes of oil equivalent

Renewables include : Biomass, Tide, Wind, Solar, Geothermal

Source: IEA – Key World Energy Statistics - 2009

The amount of total primary energy supply in million tonnes of oil equivalent (Mtoe) had a 97 percent increase over 34 years (from 1973 to 2007). The amount of renewables made a significant contribution, but not enough to cope with the overall increase to make any contribution towards increasing its share of the overall composition of the fuel supply mix.

The global community needs to do much more to mitigate greenhouse gas emissions.

Based on the prevailing trend and current policies, IEA projected that by 2030, the world will still be dependent on carbon-based fossil fuels for 80 percent of its energy demand (see Figure 3.13). More alarming is the fact that the percentage of coal/peat will increase by 2.3 percent. This trend is not healthy for the global community.

The world will be closely watching the results of the 15th United Nations Climate Change Conference (COP15), which took place in Copenhagen from 7 to 18 December 2009.

Meanwhile, IEA used a plausible scenario of a post-2010 climate policy framework to stabilise the greenhouse gases at 450 ppm CO_2-equivalent (see Figure 3.14). Figure 3.15 shows

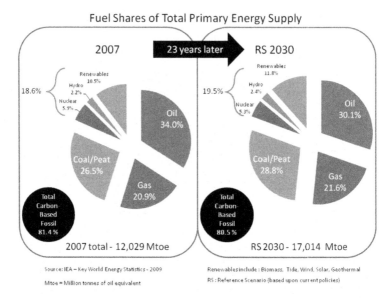

Figure 3.13: Shares of total primary energy supply by fuel type for 2007 and RS 2030 (RS: Reference Scenario base on current policies).

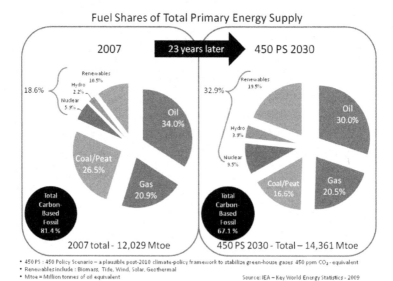

Figure 3.14: Shares of total primary energy supply by fuel type for 2007 and 450 PS 2030 (450 PS : 450 Policy Scenario — a plausible post 2010 climate policy framework to stabilize greenhouse gases at 450 ppm CO_2-equivalent).

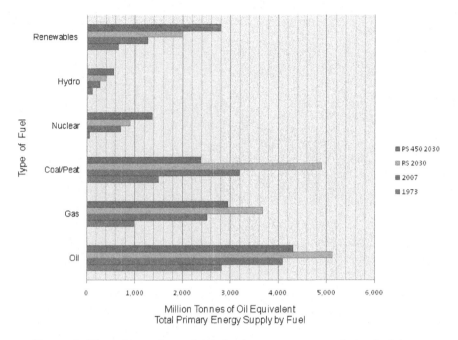

Figure 3.15: Comparison of total primary energy supply by fuel type.

the breakdown of demand for energy by fuel type in both RS 2030 and 450 PS 2030, and Figure 3.16 reflects the increasing energy requirements of the world.

In this 450 PS 2030 scenario, the carbon-based fossil fuel will have to decrease from 81.4 percent to 67.1 percent. Correspondingly, the percentage of renewables will have to almost double from 10.5 percent to 19.5 percent. In addition, the share of the nuclear option will have to increase from 5.9 percent to 9.5 percent.

The key global energy research challenge is to be able to make the major global shift from the dependence on carbon-based fossil fuel to low-carbon technologies!

Few hard truths:

- Energy demand is increasing. By 2050, the world could be using double the amount of energy that it is using today.

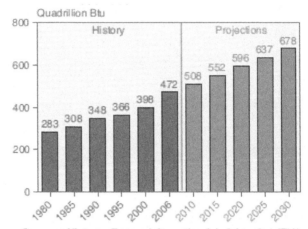

Sources: **History:** Energy Information Administration (EIA), *International Energy Annual 2006* (June-December 2008), web site www.eia.doe.gov/iea. **Projections:** EIA, World Energy Projections Plus (2009).

Figure 3.16: Increasing trend in the global need for more energy.

- World population without electricity in 2008: 1.5 billion.
- Projected world population without electricity by 2030: 1.3 billion.
- We should stop relying on "easy fossil fuel oil and gas" supplies.
- Greenhouse gas emissions are rising faster than the demand for energy.

The facts mentioned above show that more transformative energy research and innovations are urgently required to mitigate not only the greenhouse emission effect on global climate change but also other societal challenges as shown in Figure 3.17.

The Energy Research Challenge facing mankind is leadership in novel research on low-carbon energy, policy-making, business. The society should work towards a same direction of balanced transition from the current state a more sustainable planet Earth and not go beyond the Earth's carrying capacity.

Figure 3.17: Energy research challenge — solutions that are socially, environmentally and economically sustainable.

The energy research areas for the Global Research Foundation initiative could well be a multi-disciplinary research that focus on the following:

- Clean, economic and sustainable means of energy conversion, storage and distribution that can be deployed in developing and industrialised countries
- New and efficient energy conversion technologies based on renewable energy sources
- Engineering advances in fuels, combustion and thermal sciences to provide a fundamental basis for progress in meeting the energy challenge
- Making solar thermal energy conversion, solar power, wind power, and other renewable energy systems more economical

- Biomass, or bioenergy, as a versatile energy resource that can be used for industry, power generation and energy-dense transportation biofuels
- Nuclear safety and security

Renewables

In the 21st century, research in renewable or alternative energy is of utmost importance to the sustainability of our environment and the global climate. Almost all the countries in the world have been constantly reviewing their energy scenarios to have access to energy security, affordability and sustainability. Invariably, innovations that will help in the shift towards an increased percentage of renewable energy sources will be an important strategy to pursue. New knowledge and discovery in the renewable energy research frontier will provide a better strategy towards the goal of ensuring social, environment and economic sustainability.

With the exception of biomass power, there are at least two Asia Pacific countries in the top five of all the different categories of renewable energy in 2008 (see Table 3.8).

China has set an ambitious goal to generate 10 percent of its electricity supply via renewable energy sources by 2010 and 15 percent by 2020. To reach this goal, China committed to invest $12 billion in renewable energy in 2007.

For its energy strategy in the transportation sector, China will invest more than $1 trillion to expand its railway network by 50 percent by 2020. Over the next decade, China will probably be the country that will invest the most in energy development and innovation.

Wind

The earliest method of utilising wind power was the sail boat. The use of sail boats could be traced back to the

Table 3.8: 2008 renewable capacity in top five countries.

Top Five Countries	#1	#2	#3	#4	#5
Existing Capacity as of end-2008					
Renewables power capacity	China	USA	Germany	Spain	India
Small Hydro	China	Japan	USA	Italy	Brazil
Wind Power	USA	Germany	Spain	China	India
Biomass Power	USA	Brazil	Philippines	Germany	
				Sweden	
				Finland	
Geothermal power	USA	Philippines	Indonesia	Mexico	Italy
Solar PV (Grid-connected)	Germany	Spain	Japan	USA	S.Korea
Solar hot water/heating	China	Turkey	Germany	Japan	Israel

Romans and Egyptians in the 3000 B.C. era. By innovating along the same concept as the sail, windmills were designed to provide mechanical energy to mill the grains to flour for the making of bread and other forms of food and to pump water from below the ground. The first documented windmill dated as far as 1219 A.D., and Yehlu Chu-Tshai of China was recorded as the inventor of the windmill to grind grains and pump water. In Europe, the Dutch popularised the use of windmills for the grinding of grains, irrigation and drainage, sawing-milling of timber and processing of spices from the East.

The use of the windmill to generate electricity began only in around 1888 in Ohio, USA. Charles F. Brush called this windmill the Brush postmill, which was able to produce 12 kilowatts of power.

Europe, Denmark, Germany, and France continued innovating windmill technologies and called the windmills designed for electric power "wind turbines".

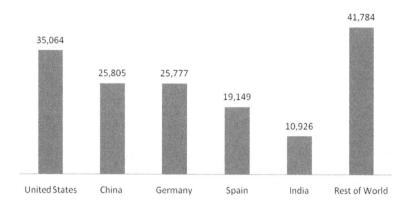

Figure 3.18: Top five countries that cumulatively installed wind power in 2009.[40]

The "1973 Oil Crisis" that lasted from October 1973 to March 1974 spurred the USA to invest in wind energy research as an alternate energy source. Governments in Europe also embarked on the development of multi-megawatt wind turbines.

As of 2009, the top five wind power countries were the USA, China, Germany Spain and India.

As seen in Table 3.8 and Figure 3.18, China became the second largest wind power country within one year! In 2009, these five countries installed a total of 28,566 MW of new wind power capacity representing 77 percent of the total share of the new additions. And we see that China had the largest share of the new additions!

We are seeing a shift of wind power technologies to the Asia Pacific region!

Solar

There have been significant developments in the way solar power is being used. With the availability of long stretches of

---

[40] Source: Global Wind Energy Council, www.gwec.net.

Table 3.9: Renewable energy: Biofuels innovations — number of patents in 2003, 2008 and 16 months period (January 2008 to April 2009).[41]

	2003	2008	16 months (January 2008 to April 2009)
Innovations in Biofuels	341 (70% patented by Japanese companies; 31% were filed in Japan)	1,878	2466 China shared top position with Japan (31% of patents were filed in China)
Harnessing Green Algae as Biofuel Patents	3	63	92

Source: Thomson Reuters.

land in China, especially in the sparsely inhabited western part of the country, the conditions for the development of solar energy are very favourable.

In the urban areas, China has made solar panels easily accessible to the masses, and today, stands at number one position in the world in terms of solar hot water/heating (see Table 3.9).

Turkey stands at number two position, Germany at third, Japan at fourth and Israel at fifth in this area.

Biofuels

The first generation of biofuels was made from sugar, starch, vegetable oils or animal fats. The second generation of biofuels was made from waste mass from non-food crops such as stalks of wheat and corn cobs. The third generation of biofuels focuses on the potential of using algae.

---

[41] Global Patenting Activity measured in DWPI (The Derwent World Patent Index), Thomas Reuters.

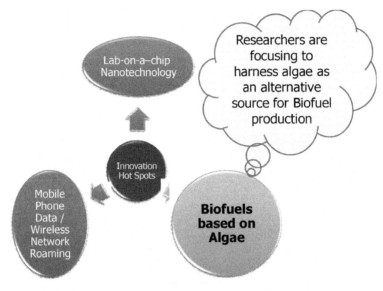

Reference: IP Market Report – Mining Patent Data for Tomorrow's Breakthrough (Thomson Reuters)

Figure 3.19: Global innovation hot spots.

Source: Thomson Reuters

Biofuels can be used for electricity generation as well as gasoline replacement or supplement.

There have been novel innovations that use micro-algae for carbon capture from gasified coal (see Figure 3.19). ENN,[42] a clean-energy company based in China, has been working on these innovations.

The Algal Carbon Capture innovations by ENN are based on clean technology approach with a bioreactor to grow micro-algae using carbon captured from gasified coal. The carbon dioxide produced is extracted by using solar or wind power. The carbon dioxide is fed into the bioreactor to grow micro-algae. Different types of micro-algae are being evaluated to find the species that is most effective in using the carbon dioxide waste. The carbon dioxide waste can come from burning coal or other carbon

---

[42] Website: http://www.enn.cn/en/about/enn_profile.html.

sources. The algae is then harvested daily to be converted into biofuels, fertilisers and animal feed (see Figure 3.19).

This Algal Carbon Capture technology is now being used by different industries in different countries. One of India's leading cement producers has adopted this technology in their cement manufacture process to capture carbon dioxide generated by cement kilns. The gas produced from the micro-algae is used as fuel in its cement kilns.

As seen in Table 3.8, under renewable power capacity there were no Asia Pacific countries among the top five countries in 2008. By 2009, as seen in Table 3.10, the ranking of biomass and biofuel research showed the three top universities in China and one top university in Japan being ranked among the top 20 universities! It is easy to conclude that the Asia Pacific

Table 3.10: Biomass and biofuel research rankings.

Rank	Institute	Country	Articles, reviews, conference papers	Average citations by publication
1	Chinese Academy of Sciences	China*	1135	1.79
2	USDA Agricultural Research Service	USA	462	3.24
3	University of Florida	USA	312	2.83
4	Universidade de Sao Paulo	Brazil	302	3.33
5	Zhejiang University	China*	296	1.81
6	Wageningen University	Netherlands	286	3.81
7	UC Davis	USA	280	3.87
8	Russian Academy of Sciences	Russia	264	1.29
9	Sveriges lantbruksuniversitet	Sweden	261	4.26
10	Oregon State University	USA	248	6.38
11	University of British Columbia	Canada	229	4.73
12	Lunds Universitet	Sweden	223	5.04
13	Michigan State University	USA	221	5.44
14	Cornell University	USA	209	5.31
15	Tsinghua University	China*	206	2.70
16	USDA Forest Service	USA	204	4.19
17	Iowa State University	USA	204	2.75
18	University of Tokyo	Japan*	200	3.45
19	Universiteit Gent	Belgium	197	4.48
20	Consiglio Nazionale delle Ricerche	Italy	194	3.63

Table 1 – Most prolific institutes in biomass and biofuel research; publication and citation years: 2005–2008.
Source: Scopus

Note: *Denotes Asia-Pacific countries.

countries, especially China and Japan, are finding new knowledge and solutions for renewable energy (see Table 3.9).

Innovators from all over the world are racing towards energy-efficient improvements, finding new sources of renewables and reducing greenhouse gas emissions through the accelerated deployment of existing and emerging energy technologies.

Current and future investments in energy in R&D activities will determine the outcome in meeting the increasing demand for energy for economic and societal developments for the growing world population.

Asia is taking the lead in many of the innovations in energy research that are relevant to its local geography and available natural resources, in order to ensure continued growth and prosperity. Leading industries in energy in USA and Europe are setting up R&D bases in Asia Pacific. All these developments will continue to build momentum for more global research collaboration in the area of sustainable energy research and developments.

3.7 FOOD SUPPLIES, NUTRITION AND FOOD SAFETY

The first goal of the UN Millennium Goals is to eradicate extreme hunger and poverty. This is in recognition of the fact that feeding the world in the 21st century will be one of mankind's greatest challenges. Given widespread land degradation, increasing population, rapidity of urbanisation, water shortages, rising energy costs and issues related to climate change, more coordinated research needs to be done.

Severe weather pattern changes such as extreme drought and floods, which are attributed to global warming, are impacting food production, distribution and prices around the world.

124

Diverting food production to biofuels is another reason behind the rise of food prices. Due to the increasing distance between the source of production and consumption of food, preservation of the nutritional value and safe handling of food become major issues as well.

In addition to social and political initiatives, feeding the world will require more investment in research so as to spread the new findings more quickly to the farmers for them to increase food production, nutritional value, safety and economics.

Food Supplies and Food Prices

The amount of food produced over the years has been increasing. However, there is a gap between the rate of increase in production and the rate of increase in population. Furthermore, the geographic areas where there are increases in food production are not found in the areas that have the greatest increase in population. Africa has the highest rate of population growth, however, due to civil conflict and weather extremes, food production has been declining.

Since 2000, the price of food around the world has increased and the price of many food items such as rice has more than doubled. The average annual price of rice in year 2000 was US$ 207 per metric ton, and increased to US$ 697 per metric ton in 2008 (about 3.4 times more). Figure 3.20 shows that average annual price of white rice, Thai 100 percent B Second Grade, f.o.b. Bangkok had more than doubled in price from 334 US$ per metric ton in 2007 to 697 US$ per metric ton in 2008.[43] Figure 3.21 displays similar trend in the price of wheat from USA.

The recent runaway increases in food prices is in turn causing malnutrition and food crisis in several regions, particularly Africa.

---

[43] Source: Jackson Son & co (London) Ltd.

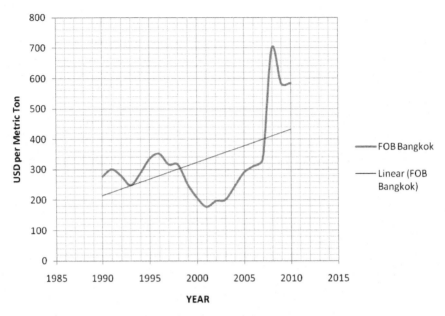

Figure 3.20: Annual average price of rice (white rice, Thai 100 percent B Second Grade (f.o.b.) Bangkok).

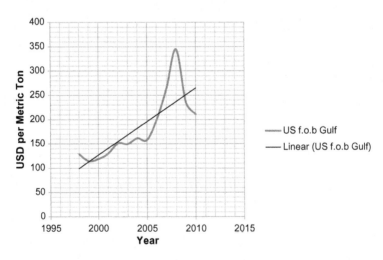

Figure 3.21: Annual average price of wheat (US No. 2, Hard Red Winter ord. Prot), US Fob Gulf.

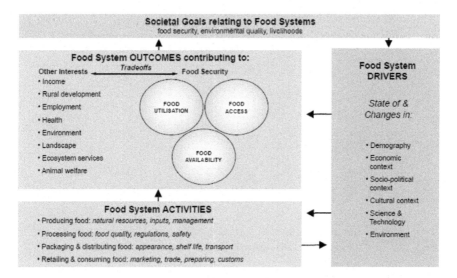

Figure 3.22: Food system — one of the food systems drivers is Science and Technology.[44]

Malnutrition in turn increases health risks. The interaction between these developments is presented in Figure 3.22.

Trend in Global Investment in Agricultural Research and Development

Overall, there is a decreasing trend in investment in agricultural research worldwide. However, in terms of percentage investment, Asia is still investing more than the rest of the world by almost two-fold (see Figure 3.23).

With the encroaching and spreading of urbanisation into rural areas, agricultural land will need to be more productive. In recent years, these has been a decline in the yield and growth of most crops. One way to address this issue is to conduct more research to discover better technology that can increase the yield of food crops.

---

[44] Ericksen, P.J. (2008) Conceptualizing Food Systems for Global Environmental Change Research. *Global Environmental Change* **18**, 234–245.

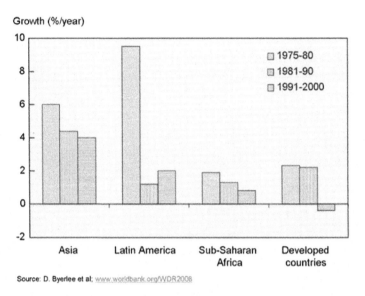

Source: D. Byerlee et al; www.worldbank.org/WDR2008

Figure 3.23: Public investment in agricultural research and development.

One key reason for the reduction in funding was that food crops are treated as a commodity. When rice prices declined steadily in the 1990s, it led many governments and agencies to believe that the supply of food was plentiful. The margins of the traders were lowered and private funding by private enterprises was also reduced.

There were several factors that caused the price hikes in 2008. The demand for grain, the basic staple of mankind, is rising rapidly with the increase in population. The growing economy in developing countries, especially China and India, resulted in more middle income people consuming more meat. The last factor is the use of food crops for biofuels.

Food crops such as maize, sugar, oilseeds and palm oil as the biomass for biofuels has increased the demand for agricultural products. Agricultural production is unable to keep up with the demand. When demand exceeds supply, prices increase. Agricultural experts had warned the developed countries of this scenario, but the warnings were ignored.

The world has to face this societal challenge of reducing hunger and undernourishment and there is still much work to be done. The situation is serious. However, there is still hope. One key solution is to increase investment in research and development in the studies that can help to increase crop yields, disease-resistant crops, crops that can be grown in marginal farmland, and develop second-generation liquid biofuels using cellulosic biomass so that the use for food crops for first-generation liquid biofuels can be decreased. The next key solution is to have a knowledge and skills transfer system so that existing and new technologies can reach farmers and countries that need them most.

On an average, the time span from discovery to application takes about 15 to 20 years. There is an urgency in rolling out existing high-yielding varieties to farmers, and provide a support system for access to fertilisers, water and environmentally-friendly pesticides which they need.

Rice is the staple food for almost half of the world's population. The biggest collection of various types of rice is held in Asia at the International Rice Research Institute (IRRI).[45] IRRI is working with many partners and collaborating with universities around the world to perform research and development that is suits local conditions. Meanwhile, IRRI is also rolling out appropriate rice seeds to the farmers in the Asian region.

Focusing on research to keep yields rising ahead of demand is a good step towards reducing hunger and malnutrition. The brown leafhopper is a major pest in Southeast Asia. IRRI scientists are developing rice plants that are resistant to the brown leafhopper and crops that can photosynthesise

---

[45] Established in 1960, IRRI is one of the largest non-profit agricultural research centres in Asia, with headquarters in the Philippines and offices in 14 nations. IRRI's mission is to reduce poverty and hunger, improve the health of rice farmers and consumers, and ensure that rice production is environmentally sustainable.

more efficiently. These crops, which are called C_4, are found in plants such as maize. They hope to double rice yields and cut down the plants' need for nitrogen (fertiliser) and water.

Harnessing all available agricultural technologies and using them for sustainable urban agriculture will be another major area that the R&D community can focus on. The creative use of "fringe" land in urban areas can be aesthetically developed for urban agriculture by "smallholders" who may be active senior citizens (above 60 years old). This may be a synergistic approach to taking care of food security and addressing the societal challenge of ageing populations.

Nutrition

Having an understanding of the role of food as a nutrient source for humans will make a major difference in our lives.

Global climate change, air, water and soil pollution, and modern farming practices with chemical fertilisers have depleted our soil of vital minerals. In processed food, there is widespread use of chemicals, food additives, salt, sugar and transfat. The modern-day diet contains a high proportion of processed foods that are linked to many diseases such as cardiovascular diseases, cancer, arthritis and osteoporosis.

For the first time, in 2009, more than one billion people were hungry and undernourished (see Figures 3.24 and 3.25).[46]

"A dangerous mix of the global economic slowdown combined with stubbornly high food prices in many countries has pushed some 100 million more people than last year into chronic hunger and poverty. The silent hunger crisis — affecting one-sixth of all of humanity — poses a serious risk for world

---

[46] *The State of Food Insecurity in the World 2009*, FAO, Rome 2009.

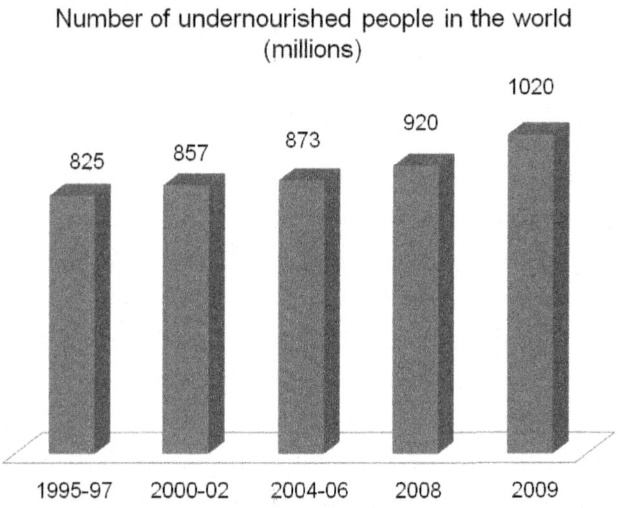

Number of undernourished people in the world
(millions)

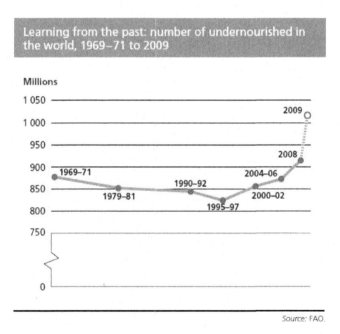

Source : FAO

Figure 3.24: Undernourishment has been increasing since 1995.

**Learning from the past: number of undernourished in
the world, 1969–71 to 2009**

Source: FAO.

Figure 3.25: Estimated number of undernourished people in the world.

peace and security. " — FAO Director-General Jacques Diouf (19 June 2009, Rome).

Poor agricultural practices that use environmentally-unfriendly chemicals and pesticides, poor agricultural infrastructure, natural disasters, extreme weather, conflict and poverty are major causes for people being hungry and undernourished. In 2009, when more than one billion people went hungery, the reason was attributed to high food prices and the global economic crisis.

People who are hungry and undernourished will have micronutrient deficiencies. These deficiencies can make people more susceptible to health problems such as infectious diseases, impaired physical growth and mental development. All these can reduce the life expectancy and labour productivity of a country.

The scientific communities in industries, universities and government agencies can play an important role in conducting research and development to help reduce undernourishment in the entire food chain — from farm to fork.

New innovations will help areas with shortages of land or water, or with unique local or regional problems of soil or climate. Often, these are the areas with a high concentration of poor people and where help is required the most.

Biotechnology research can provide means of improving food security and reducing pressures on the environment. A mission-oriented research strategy to have crops that can be farmed in poor and degraded land will greatly increase the availability of land for food production. The focus of research can be on crops and also on soil acidity and salinity, and on soil that is resistant to drought or water logging, not influenced by extreme temperatures, and pest- and disease-resistant.

The key challenge is for the new varieties to be safe for human consumption and sustainable for the environment.

How do we feed nine billion people?

We are seeing the rise of a new age of philanthropist funding for global research to find solutions to these problems.

The world will be able to feed the growing global population if the global community works together. If people regard food as a source of nutrients and as a commodity, the quality of life of people will be improved and we will have lesser number of undernourished people.

Food Safety

There are about 265 types of food-borne diseases[47] as classified by the Center of Disease Control. A summary of the categories and numbers of diseases transmitted by foods is tabulated in Table 3.11.

The severity of food-borne diseases caused by bacteria, virus, parasites, plant toxins and poisonous chemicals varies from mild stomach upsets to life-threatening symptoms and deaths.

In a recent study by Robert L. Scharff,[48] the health-related costs arising from food-borne illnesses is about US$ 152 million per annum in United States.

Table 3.11: Summary of the number and categories of diseases transmitted by food.

Type of Diseases Transmitted by Foods	Numbers of Diseases
Bacterial Diseases	53
Viral and Rickettsial Diseases	19
Parasitic Diseases	67
Plant Toxicants and Toxins	76
Poisonous Chemicals	50
Total number of Food Borne Diseases	265

[47] Bryan FL, Disease transmitted by Foods. Atlanta: Centers for Disease Control; 1982.
[48] Scharff RL, Health-Related Costs from Foodborne Illness in the United States. For the Produce Safety Project at Georgetown University, 2010.

Out of 82 million cases of food-borne diseases, 67 million are classified as those caused due to unknown agents. This would mean an economic impact of US$ 96 million. This may be a potential area for future research.

The two most prevalent food-borne diseases caused due to bacterial transmission are caused by Campylobacter spp. and Salmonella, nontyphoidal. The losses resulting from these two bacterial transmitted food-borne diseases came to US$ 18 billion.

The two most prevalent food-borne diseases due to parasitic transmission are caused by *Toxoplasma gondii* and *Giardia lamblia*. The losses resulting from these parasite-transmitted food-borne disease came to US$ 33 billion.

In the case of virally-transmitted food-borne diseases, the single organism responsible for the diseases is the Norwalk-like virus. With almost ten million cases a year, it is the second most common food-borne disease in US.

The highest cost per case is caused by *Vibrio vulnificus*, which is the leading cause of death in food-borne diseases. The most common cause of this disease is eating raw and under-cooked shellfish in areas that are contaminated by this bacteria.

There is much more that can be done to make food safe for all.

Food safety should be one of the top priorities of a country. The industrialization and automation of food production has increased the time involved in producing food until it reaches the table. Different stages in processing variety of foods namely production, distribution to final consumption have their own safety handling challenges.

The entire food chain from "farm to fork" deserves the attention of the global research community. What we eat will ultimately have a great impact on our health.

3.8   CLIMATE CHANGE

Climate change refers to the change in weather patterns because of an increase in the earth's average temperature and global warming.

Recent disasters and deaths caused by extreme weather conditions such as Hurricane Katrina in the USA, the extreme hot summer temperatures of 45 degree Celsius in Europe in July 2007 and recent droughts in China and Australia are making people from all over the world more sensitised to the issues of climate change.

Climate change has undoubtedly become a major challenge that all countries are facing today. The reason behind climate change is the greenhouse effect, where molecules of different gases trap heat in the earth's atmosphere, similar to growing plants in a greenhouse, and keep our environment warm enough to sustain life. Carbon dioxide and other "greenhouse gases" (GHGs) are an integral part of the earth's natural cycles, but human activities from agriculture, transportation, to industry are causing an imbalance by pumping up their concentrations into the atmosphere to dangerous levels. The consequence is rising global temperatures that cause unpredictable weather patterns which in turn cause disasters affecting human lives, economies and ecosystems.

The climate of the earth is governed primarily by complex interactions among the sun, oceans and atmosphere. The increased concentration of greenhouse gases in the atmosphere has led to global warming and fundamentally changed the natural process that controls the global climate.

In 2007, the UN's Intergovernmental Panel on Climate Change (IPCC) Report drew the conclusion that since the mid-20th century, "most of the increase in global warming is very likely caused by human activities".

135

The report estimated that global warming can range from 1.1 degree Celsius to 6.4 degree Celsius. This is dependent on the volume of man-made greenhouse gases that continues to be emitted into the atmosphere.

Table 3.12 shows different greenhouse gases listed by IPCC. It is interesting to note that it is not just carbon dioxide that is emitted, other greenhouse gases include methane, nitrous oxide and fluoro gases such as hydrofluoro-carbons, perfluoro-carbons and sulphur hexa-fluoride.

In Table 3.13, the IPCC provided a list of human activities that are sources of greenhouse gases. The different types of human activities in decreasing order of impact are energy

Table 3.12:   Types of greenhouse gases.

Global Emissions of Greenhouse Gases

The primary human generated greenhouse gases and their sources

Carbon dioxide	Fossil fuel combustion Land clearing for agriculture Cement production	
Methane	Livestock production Extraction of fossil fuels Rice cultivation Landfills Sewage	
Nitrous oxide	Industrial processes Fertilizer use	
Fluoro gases	Hydrofluoro-carbons	Leakages from refrigerators, aerosols, air conditioners
	Perfluoro-carbons	Aluminium production Semi-conductor industry
	Sulphur Hexa-Fluoride	Electrical insulation Magnesium smelting

Source: IPCC.

Table 3.13: List of human activities that are sources of greenhouse gases.

Greenhouse gas sources by sector of human activities	
Source of greenhouse gas	Sector
Energy supply	Electricity and centralized heat generation, Resource extraction (Oil and Gas exploration and production) Grid based transmission/distribution
Industry	Production of metals, Pulp and paper manufacture Cement production Chemicals manufacture Petroleum refining
Forestry	Deforestation Decomposition of biomass that remains after logging
Agriculture	Crop and livestock production
Transportation	Travel by car, freight truck, plane, train or ship
Residential and commercial buildings	Heating, cooling and electricity
Waste	Landfills Incineration Wastewater

Source: IPCC

supply, industry, forestry, agriculture, transport, buildings and waste respectively.

It is interesting to observe in Table 3.14 that giving carbon dioxide the reference level of one in global warming potential, other greenhouse gases have higher multiples of global warming potential. This broadens our understanding that it is not just carbon dioxide emissions into the atmosphere that we have to be concerned with, but also many other greenhouse gases that have a significant impact on climate change. Global research will need

Table 3.14: Global warming potential of selected greenhouse gases.

Global Warming Potential (GWP) expresses a gas's heat-trapping power relative to carbon dioxide over a particular time period (In this table, IPCC, uses the common 100-year time frame).

Greenhouse Gas	Global Warming Potential
Carbon Dioxide	1
Methane	25
Nitrous Oxide	298
Hydrofluorocarbons	124 – 14,800
Perfluorocarbons	7,390 – 12,200
Sulphur Hexafluoride	22,800

Graphic representation below show the relative GWP using median numbers

Source : IPCC

to focus on the fluoro-based greenhouse gases and find new ways to mitigate their emissions and impact on climate change.

In Figure 3.26, the 2007 data from the Carbon Dioxide Information Analysis Centre[49] (CDIAC) shows that the top three emitters of carbon dioxide with reference to regions are China, the USA and the EU-27 respectively. The top three countries based on emission per person are USA, Canada and Russia. Statistics show that wealthier nations emit more carbon dioxide per person than the less wealthy ones.

In Figure 3.27, we see that during the 57-year period, the top two nations that had emitted the biggest portion of global

---

[49] Website: http://cdiac.ornl.gov/.

Top 10 CO$_2$-Emitting Nations, Total and Per Person, 2007

National emissions levels vary greatly. Among the top 10 emitters, China generates nearly 15 times more CO$_2$ than Mexico does. The 10 leading emitters generate many more times the emissions of most developing countries, although emissions in those countries are rising rapidly and could soon overtake the annual emissions in industrial countries. The top 10 emitting nations also exhibit a broad range of emissions per person. Wealthy countries tend to emit more carbon dioxide per person than poor countries do.

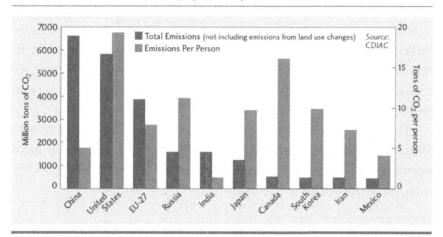

Figure 3.26:   2007 data of the top ten carbon dioxide emitting nations.

Top 10 CO$_2$-Emitting Nations' Share of Global CO$_2$ Emissions, 1950–2007

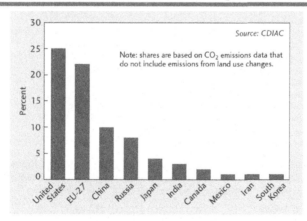

Figure 3.27:   Share of global carbon dioxide emission from the top ten CO$_2$-emitting nations from 1950 to 2007.

Source: CDIAC.

emission are USA and EU-27 respectively. China is the third and its emission level is 40 percent of USA.

The impact and severity of the global climate change varies from country to country. Different parts of the world will experience more heat waves, floods, droughts storms and hurricanes. Food crops' yield will fall, some areas will have water shortages, others will have floods, the ecosystems in the sea and land will have less biodiversity and some species may even face extinction. Climate change affects the poorest and least developed countries more severely than others.

It is probably easier to conjure up images of battered coast-lines, flooded roads, extreme temperatures as the world gets warmer; we hardly associate diseases and health implications with climate change.

From Rotterdam to Yokohama (Japan) via	Distance (KM)	Distance (Miles)
Suez Canal (Southerly route)	20,750	12,894
Northeast Passage	13,602	8,452
Distance Shortened by	7,148	4,442

Figure 3.28: The Northeast Passage and distance saved using the northeast passage instead of the Suez Canal. (The Russian Ministry of Transport)

New emerging evidence on the health impact of climate change indicates future challenges. Scientists and researchers will need to find solutions to address these problems. The challenges will involve identifying, quantifying and predicting the health impacts that are of global scale. Epidemiologists usually undertake studies that are geographically localised.

Several vector-borne infectious diseases are dependent on rainy or dry seasons to spread quickly. The extension of wet or dry seasons will have direct and indirect impacts on human health. Extensive flooding will increase the severity of water-borne diseases.

Tibet's vast glaciers and high altitude of the Himalayan mountains are the source of one of the world's greatest river systems that is shared by several countries. China and India are two countries that have river sources which also flow through Bangladesh, Myanmar, Bhutan, Nepal, Cambodia, Pakistan, Laos, Thailand and Vietnam. The river systems provide water to about 47 percent of the global population.

Keeping in view the Tibetan glacier, China and India recognise the threat of global warming due to climate change. In August 2009, China and India started to discuss a joint research study on the impact of climate change on the glaciers in the Himalayan and Tibetan regions. The discussion included the institutionalisation of collaboration between China's Cold and Arid Regions Environmental and Engineering Research and The Wadia Institute of Himalayan Geology, India. India recognises that China has invested significant human resources in the study of glaciology whereas it had started such studies only recently. A joint research has the advantage of a more in-depth and bigger geographical area to study the impact of climate change.

China and India have recently signed a Glacier Research collaboration to study the impact of receding Tibetan glaciers.

Climate change on Earth affects every human being. A global societal challenge involving the whole planet needs a global community to come together to find solutions or ways to mitigate further damages.

A global research foundation with the right funding and participation from the international community of researchers and all stakeholders is the need of the hour.

Climate Change Impact at the Arctic

For centuries, mariners have searched for a shortcut between the Atlantic and Pacific oceans through the Arctic. For the first time in the summer of 2009, two German cargo ships were able to transit this Northeast Passage that was enabled by the impact of global warming on the melting of the Arctic ice.

The Northeast Passage is the sea lane that extends from Europe's North Sea, along the Arctic coast of the Asian continent and through the Bering Sea to the Pacific Ocean.

Global warming is a phenomenon that always has a negative impact. However, the melting ice in the Northeast Passage and the possibility to sail through the Arctic Ocean seems to have an unintended positive effect. The Northeast Passage across the Arctic Ocean provides a shorter journey than travelling through the Suez Canal, and thus will lead to energy savings and the reduction of carbon dioxide and other gas emissions. The difference in the length of the voyage from Europe via Suez to the Pacific compared to that via Panama to the Atlantic is rather significant.

The voyage from Rotterdam to Yokohama (Japan) via Suez is 20,751 kilometres whereas the voyage via Northeast Passage is 13,602 kilometres. This translates to a 34 percent reduction in distance travelled. Saving on a distance of 7,149 kilometres can save about 13 days of sea travel.

The voyage from Rotterdam to Shanghai (China) via Suez is 19,484 kilometres whereas the voyage via Northeast Passage is 14,962 kilometres. This translates to a 23 percent reduction in distance travelled. Saving on a distance of 4,522 kilometres can save about eight days of sea travel.

The voyage from Rotterdam to Vancouver (Canada) via Panama is 16,515 kilometres whereas the voyage via Northeast Passage is 12,936 kilometres. This translates to a 22 percent reduction in distance travelled. Saving on a distance of 3,579 kilometres can save about six days of sea travel.

With the melting of the Arctic icecap, scientists are finding evidence on the presence of oil in seabeds samples 200 miles from the North Pole. According to the United States Geological Survey, one quarter of the world's undiscovered oil and gas resources may be available in the Arctic.

Keeping in view the above facts, global collaboration to perform research associated with the melting of glaciers and ice caps in the Arctic is gaining more significance.

The interconnected world needs all its combined knowledge and talent to cope with the impacts of climate change that we are observing and also more research to prevent further climate change for the benefit of future generations.

3.9   AGEING

The speed of demographic ageing across the world is accelerating, especially in Asia Pacific. Using the yardstick of years taken for the number of people over the age of 65 to increase from 7 percent to 14 percent of a country's population, France's ageing process in took 115 years. On the other hand, in the ageing process Asia Pacific countries such as China, Japan, Singapore, Sri Lanka and Thailand took less than 30 years (see Figure 3.29). The ageing population trend is irreversible as the proportion of young people will not be able to

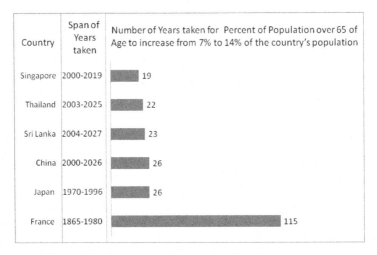

Figure 3.29: Comparison of the speed of demographic ageing of selected Asia Pacific countries with France.

catch up due to the increased life expectancy and declining birth rates.

Ageing is one of the greatest challenges facing humanity in this century. Within the next 50 years, most nations, except major parts of the African continent, will have 20 percent or more of people of 65 years and above.

We can say that some 200 years ago, the world was young. However, by 2050, we will be in the "Aged World". This is largely due to longer life expectancy as a result of better sanitation, healthcare, agricultural practices, industrialisation and major advances in science and technology.

In Table 3.15, we estimated that in a 100-year period, the number of people age 65 and above will increase by 1,315 million or 11.5 times!.

Table 3.15 clearly shows that with the global increase in population, the only decreasing trend is the segment of the population aged below 19.

To put this into a visual perspective, a joint study of Ageing into the 21st Century by the United Nations University and

Table 3.15: The world population distribution by age group projected to year 2050.[50]

Age Group	Year 1950 Million	%	Year 2000 Million	%	Year 2050 Million	%	Trend
65+	125	5	420	7	1,440	16	Increasing
20-64	1,275	51	3,240	54	5,130	57	Increasing
0-19	1,100	44	2,340	39	2,430	27	Decreasing
Total	2,500	100	6,000	100	9,000	100	Increasing

WHO Kobe Center stated that, "every month, more than a million people turn 60".[51]

Global life expectancy has risen due to better hygiene and sanitation, scientific and technological advances in healthcare, industrialisation, socio-economic developments and improved communications.

The world is facing the twin phenomenon of the accelerated speed of ageing and a dramatic increase in the number of people above 60 years of age.

The highest life expectancy is in Japan with an average of 83 years. It also has the highest healthy life expectancy of 72 years for men and 78 years for women. There is much we can learn from Japan on how to obtain the highest healthy life expectancy in a society.

The Grand Challenge of Ageing Society

Good health is essential for older people to remain mobile and independent in order for them to be able to play an active part in their families and communities.

---

[50] Source: Population Division of the Department of Economic and Social Affairs of the United Nations Secretariat, World Population Prospects: The 2006 Revision and World Urbanization Prospects: The 2005 Revision, http://esa.un.org/unpp.

[51] Ageing Societies, http://wisdom.unu.edu/en/ageing-societies/.

Preventive medicine has an important role to play in this. When prevention fails, intervention will have to take place. Due to the rapid growth of Asia's ageing population, there is a need to accelerate the rate of investments into R&D that is concerned with the prevention or cure of diseases selated to ageing. Asia is badly in need of research on ageing.

In 2009, Japan had more than 20 percent of its population aged 65 years and above, and this is expected to reach about 33 percent, or one in every three people, by 2025.

Some Key Innovation Initiatives for Ageing in Japan

Japan leads the world in industrial robotics design and research. Japan recognises the trend of rapidly ageing populations and has taken several initiatives in the area of robotics to address this societal challenge.

Research in robotic systems has been ongoing and is now penetrating many areas. These include manufacturing, medical applications, remote devices for space exploration, entertainment, security applications and personal assistance for the elderly.

Scientists are working closely with Japanese industries to design and build robots to help the elderly in performing tasks such as walking, carrying heavy loads, caring for themselves and even farming. Robotics research is now directed towards developing an interactive interface with humans to facilitate personal assistance for the elderly.

Figure 3.32 shows that research on an interactive face robot that allows humans to communicate with it in both verbal and non-verbal ways has shown progress. This kind of robot can be used in both hospitals and at home.

It is expected that by 2025, there could be five million people being hospitalised. Thus, researchers are developing nurse robots and teacher robots that will be able to have human-like facial expressions in order to lend these robots a human touch.

University students demonstrating "exo-skeleton" or "robot suit" that helps aged farmers to carry heavy load ➡

Models wearing "exo-skeleton" or "robot suit" demonstrating walking up and down stairs ⬇

⬆

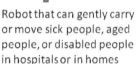

Robot that can gently carry or move sick people, aged people, or disabled people in hospitals or in homes

Figure 3.30: Robotics research initiatives in Japan for the ageing population.

Japan has been contributing many innovative solutions in the area of robotics to meet the global societal challenge of ageing populations (Figure 3.30).

The above examples demonstrate the use of robots, designed by cutting-edge technology to address social problems such as caring for the aged. The focus of robotics research is based on the ergonomics of Asian human characteristics. It will be good if there is a global research centre so that there will be no duplication of new research findings.

Research on Ageing in Singapore

By taking a biological approach towards solving ageing issues, Singapore has discovered how ageing could perhaps be delayed. A team of scientists in Singapore found that by reducing the levels of p38MAPK (a protein), the multiplication of ageing tissues can be delayed. This discovery has provided insight into the molecular mechanism of the ageing process, and has also led to the discovery of new ways of treating Type 2 diabetes in elderly people.[52]

It is necessary for a Global Innovation Community to be set up in order to discover new innovations to address the needs of the ageing society.

The desired outcome is to:

- Improve the quality of life of elderly people and their family and care givers;
- Make health and social services sustainable; and
- Create new jobs and new business opportunities for industries.

So far, most of the research and development initiatives on ageing are very much focused on national needs. The challenge is to create a global innovation community on ageing that is closely intertwined with healthcare, human resources, economics, science and technology.

In order to focus on the benefits of increased life expectancy, enhanced health and a better quality of life, we will need to adopt an integrated, multi-national approach to our policy-making in this area. Such a change in mindset will be a major paradigm shift for the better.

The goal of an international research community will be to discover innovative solutions so that we can all still enjoy a quality life that is productive and meaningful in our old age.

3.10   HEALTHCARE

Global expenditure on healthcare was about 8.7 percent of Gross Domestic Product (GDP) in 2006. The USA spent the highest at

---

[52] Source: http://www.straitstimes.com/Breaking%2BNews/Singapore/Story/ STIStory_405945.html.

Table 3.16: The state of health (illnesses) on 9 April 2009.

Illnesses and Injury Incidences	
Population living with AIDS	34,438,360
HIV/AIDS Infections	5,639,399
Cancer	6,276,384
TB	5,152,661
Syphilis	6,318,221
Chlamydia	29,416,391
Gonorrhoea	25,602,133
Childhood Diseases	51,577,605
Hepatitis	1,078,802
Malaria	275,822,998
Respiratory Infections	304,594,765
Maternal Conditions	19,485,580
Nutritional Deficiences	37,297,842
Diabetes	7,860,549
Cardiovascular Diseases	10,300,714
Asthma	12,033,257
Traffic Accidents	14,026,486
Population Living with Autism	101,525,791
Autism Diagnosis	1,398,550

Source: http://www.poodwaddle.com/worldclock.swf

12.8 percent of GDP, while the Southeast Asia Region spent the lowest at 3.4 percent of GDP (World Health Statistics 2009).

Table 3.16 shows the likely numbers of people around the world afflicted with various diseases on 9 April 2009.

The four major global health challenges that have been identified are:

1. The possibility of an outbreak of another pandemic, such as H1N1, SARS (Severe Acute Respiratory Syndrome), avian flu, or dengue fever;
2. The high prevalence of malaria, tuberculosis, diarrhea, and pneumonia that persists in the poorest countries;
3. The rapid growth of non-communicable diseases in developing countries, while their public health systems are still grappling with the conventional diseases of poverty; and

4. The HIV/AIDS pandemic, which continues to spread unchecked in some countries.
(Disease Control Priorities Project — Using Evidence About "Best Buys" to Advance Global Health).

Infectious Diseases

Looking at Table 3.16, respiratory infections are the most common form of illnesses.

The recent resurgence of infectious diseases such as the pandemic H1N1 Influenza in 2009 and SARS in 2003 reminded many healthcare experts of the history of lethal infectious diseases, such as the Spanish flu pandemic of 1918. Many underestimate the serious impact that flu can have on human health and the economy.

Although 20 to 50 million deaths were attributed to the 1918 Spanish flu, while only 812 deaths were attributed to SARS in 2003, the economic impact between the two was different. The virulent nature of the 1918 Spanish flu caused rather high mortality rates for people aged 18 to 40. The sudden decline of this productive age group in the population a created a long-term negative economic impact that lasted for several years. For SARS, with fewer deaths, the economic impact was immediate and global. The Asian Development Bank estimated that the economic impact of SARS in Asia amounted to about a loss of US$ 59 billion. Figure 3.31 shows the number of deaths in major world flu pandemics.

SARS started in Asia and spread globally in a short period of time. This rapidity was largely due to the high mobility of people travelling by air. The lack of preparedness and the uncoordinated response to SARS led to mass panic. People stopped travelling due to fear, and suddenly, airports became like ghost towns, while many businesses went bankrupt due to a lack of customers.

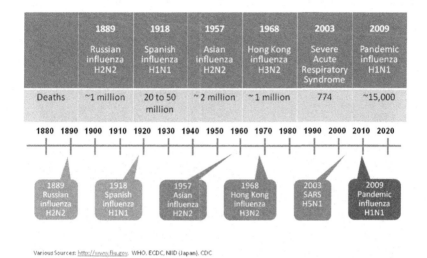

	1889	1918	1957	1968	2003	2009
	Russian influenza H2N2	Spanish influenza H1N1	Asian influenza H2N2	Hong Kong influenza H3N2	Severe Acute Respiratory Syndrome	Pandemic influenza H1N1
Deaths	~1 million	20 to 50 million	~2 million	~1 million	774	~15,000

Various Sources: http://www.flu.gov. WHO. ECDC, NIID (Japan). CDC

Figure 3.31: World flu pandemic deaths.

In 2009, the world experienced another pandemic caused by a new strain of the H1N1 influenza virus that originated from Mexico (see Figure 3.32). Originating from the Mexican state of Veracruz, it was initially referred to as the "swine flu".

The H1N1 pandemic affected every continent, regardless of healthcare standards, hygiene practices, availability of sanitation and socio-economic status (see Table 3.17). When the spread became global, each government took immediate steps to find ways to protect its citizens. In the interests of all countries, it is ideal for global collaboration to take place before another pandemic strikes. Now is the best time to commence global collaboration on how to prevent and contain any pandemic. Such measures will aid us in optimising human and financial resources in research and development.

Global Healthcare Spending

There is a huge disparity in healthcare across the world.

Figure 3.32: The H1N1 flu pandemic started in Mexico in March 2009.[53]

Table 3.17: 2009 H1N1 pandemic global deaths statistics.[54]

2009 H1N1 Flu Pandemic Global Deaths Data	
Region	Confirmed Deaths
North America	3,642
Central and South America	3,427
Asia Pacific	2,904
Europe and Central Asia	2,290
Mediterranean and Middle East	1,907
Africa	116
Global Total	14,286

---

[53] Source: http://www.mexicanflu2009.com/1900%E2%80%99s-flu-pandemics/html.

[54] Source: European Centre for Disease Prevention and Control, http://ecdc.europa.eu/en/healthtopics/H1N1/Pages/home.aspx.

In 2000, the USA had the highest healthcare spending in the world at $4,500 per person; 77 years is the life expectancy. On the other hand, Japan spent $2,000 per person and experienced a higher life expectancy of 77.2 years. Japan was able to achieve a slightly higher life expectancy despite having lower healthcare spending. Singapore spent about $2,000 per person and had a life expectancy of 78.8 years.

In some ways, Asia's healthcare model is more cost-effective than that of the USA or Europe.

HIV/AIDS

At the end of 2009, it was estimated that there were over 34 million people living with AIDS.

With the high mobility of people travelling and new lifestyles in societies, the spread and impact of HIV/AIDS will continue unabated if education on AIDS, containment of its spread, and the search for an affordable are not carried out swiftly.

The global percentage of people living with HIV seems to have stabilised since 2000, but the overall number of people living with HIV has increased. This increase is due to new infections and HIV patients surviving due to the availability of anti-retroviral therapy. Nevertheless, Sub-Saharan Africa still remains most heavily affected by HIV. In 2007, it was estimated that there were 33 million people living with HIV. Based on available data, Sub-Saharan Africa accounted for 67 percent of all people living with HIV and for 72 percent of AIDS deaths in that year.

In Asia, the estimated number of people with HIV/AIDS is about 4.7 million, and there are concerns that it will escalate. On a brighter note, Asia has seen successful large-scale HIV prevention programmes, which was resulted in Thailand and Cambodia seeing a significant decrease in HIV infection numbers.

The Global Plan to Stop Tuberculosis (TB)

TB is an infectious disease caused by mycobacteria which attacks mainly the lungs. It is easily spread through the air when an infected person coughs, spits or sneezes.

The WHO estimated that about a third of the world's population has TB, with one person being infected each second on average.

It is encouraging to see there is a global effort that aims to eradicate TB by 2050 (see Figures 3.33 and 3.34).

The Stop TB Partnership is a network of organisations and individual donors which was established in 2001.[55] Its ultimate aim is to eradicate TB so that we can have a TB-free world.

With an estimated lost of US$ 56 million, this global effort aims to save 14 million lives over the next ten years.

Government contribution (including loans) to total TB control costs by gross national income (GNI) per capita, 19 high-burden countries,[a] 2009

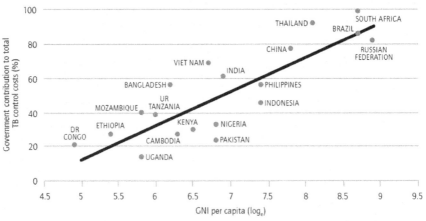

[a] Data on GNI per capita not available for Afghanistan, Myanmar and Zimbabwe.

Figure 3.33: Global effort to eradicate TB.

---

[55] Source: http://www.stoptb.org/about/accessed 6 April 2010.

Global Fund commitments for TB control by region,
as of end 2008[a]

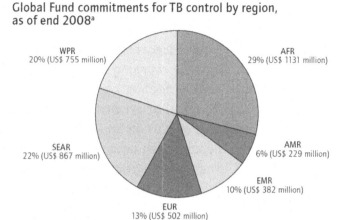

WPR
20% (US$ 755 million)

AFR
29% (US$ 1131 million)

SEAR
22% (US$ 867 million)

AMR
6% (US$ 229 million)

EMR
10% (US$ 382 million)

EUR
13% (US$ 502 million)

Proportion of estimated global incident cases of TB that are accounted for by each region

WPR 21%

AFR 31%

SEAR 34%

AMR 3%

EMR 6%

EUR 5%

[a] Refers to the total budgets approved in rounds 1-8.

Figure 3.34:   Global effort to eradicate TB.

Global Cooperation

In the area of healthcare, these is evidently a global community coming together to address and map out best practices and policies to contain pandemics of flu, HIV/AIDS and TB. However, in the area of medical research, we see countries racing each other in their bid to be the first to discover a cure.

What we need is a global pool of research talent to work together for the common good of mankind. There is an urgent need to conduct research on a global level regarding special types of diseases and health conditions in developing countries where profit-driven companies will not want to invest their resources in.

We believe that a global research community comprising international research experts working together will bring about a faster and more cost-effective response.

It is a heartening sign to see that private philanthropists, led by the Bill & Melinda Gates Foundation and Merieux Alliance,[56] are already active in the global health program. It would be better if governments and other organisations could join hands to form a Global Research Foundation that will facilitate cooperation in finding solutions to mankind's healthcare challenges.

Life expectancy has gone up, and the present levels of the quality of life and productivity need to be maintained. This will be aided by new discoveries and innovations in the areas of regenerative medicine, advanced medical devices and biotechnology. These will be key research areas that the Global Research Foundation can look into. The overall goal is to work towards new innovations that will helps us in preventing diseases, healing and restoring the health of people.

New ways to prevent diseases, heal bodies and restore them to the original state of health will be the continuing challenge that the Global Research Foundation can help to address.

---

[56] Source: http://www.stoptb.org/about/ accessed 6 April 2010.

Chapter 4

SPOILERS — INEQUITY, PROTECTIONISM AND CONFLICT

Inequity, protectionism and conflict are "spoilers" that can cause disruption to the trend of innovation.

Inequality in the distribution of resources and wealth is often a root cause of social tension and conflict. Inequity will cause even more issues should the distribution be unfair and unjust. The bigger the difference in income and wealth, the more glaring inequity will be, and the higher the potential for conflict or rebellion.

There are disparities both within a country and between nations. Within the country, the disparity often lies between the urban and rural areas. The disparity of income and wealth between nations and even regions is also of great concern.

An analysis of poverty levels based on World Bank Development Indicators statistics for 2008 showed that the disparity of wealth is a major concern. It can be a spoiler for the shift of innovation.

Although world GDP has grown, almost half of the world lives on less than US$2.50 per day (see Figure 4.1).

We see a positive trend that poverty rates have been falling, especially in East Asia and the Pacific (see Figure 4.2). However, the absolute number of moderately poor people remains almost constant at approximately 2.6 billion (see Figure 4.3). This is due to the rapid proportional increase in the global population.

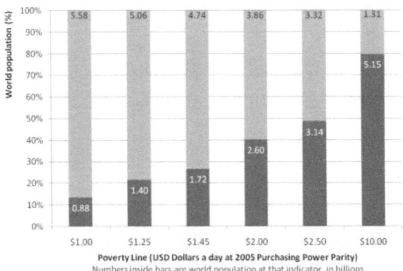

Source: World Bank Development Indicators 2008

Figure 4.1: Percentage of people in the world at different poverty levels at 2005 PPP.[57]

One key societal challenge will be to lift people out of poverty. In addition, coordinated and concerted efforts must be made to close the wide income and wealth gaps between the urban and rural populations in several regions of the world.

New innovations can be adapted and used to lift people out of the poverty cycle. However, the majority of for-profit enterprises will not find investments in research and development attractive enough to develop innovative technologies that are low-priced with low returns. The promotion of innovative technologies to bring people out of poverty will be driven mainly by governments and philanthropic organisations.

---

[57] PPP — Purchasing Power Parity.

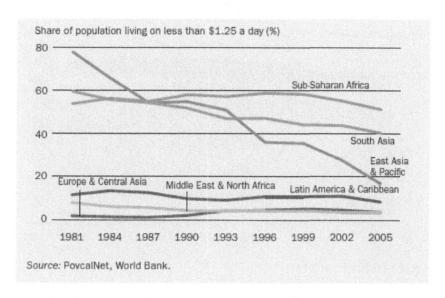

Share of population living on less than $1.25 a day (%)

Source: PovcalNet, World Bank.

Figure 4.2: Positive trend that extreme poverty[58] rates have begun to fall.

In recent years, China and India have experienced rapid economic growth. This economic growth has lifted large numbers of people above the poverty line. Paradoxically, this economic growth has widened the urban-rural income gap. The disparity in the distribution of wealth between the urban and rural population had widened since the year 2000. In 2000, the urban personal average income was 2.79 times that of the rural personal average income. By 2009, the urban personal average income had increased to four to six times that of the rural personal average income.[59]

According to an Asian Development Bank report in 2009, India had 50 billionaires (in US dollars) in a population of 1.1 billion, who

---

[58] Extreme poverty is defined as living on less than USD $1.25 (PPP) per day. Moderate poverty is defined as less than USD $2 (PPP) per day (The World Bank).
[59] The Blue Book of Cities in China — Annual Report of Urban Development of China, 2009, Chinese Academy of Social Sciences.

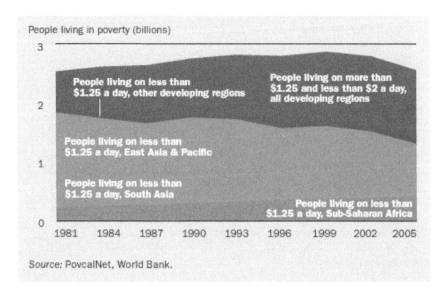

Source: PovcalNet, World Bank.

Figure 4.3: The total number of people living on less than US$2 a day remained about the same level of 2.6 billion since 1981.

controlled wealth equivalent to 20 percent of the country's gross domestic product and 80 percent of stock market capitalisation. Efforts must be made to close such a wide income gap before the disparity becomes a "time-bomb" of unrest. Research institutions can contribute by taking initiatives to engage these billionaires in philanthropic contributions towards research that will contribute significantly in lifting people out of poverty.

There has been an overall increase in global wealth. We are in an unprecedented moment in human history. Between 1999 and 2004, 135 million people were lifted out of poverty (this number is larger than the population in Japan).

However, Sub-Saharan Africa will continue to become relatively poorer compared to the rest of the world in 2025–2030. This Sub-Saharan African region is in a vicious cycle as they lack the resources to enjoy the benefits of the globalisation of trade and technology due to their existing political and economic situation.

Over the next two to three decades, the "global middle class" is projected to grow from 440 million to 1.2 billion. Most of the new entrants will be from Asia, of whom the majority will come from China and India.

The way to alleviate poverty is to bring innovation to the urban and rural population, so that economic development can be inclusive of the "poor" in order to be sustainable.

PROTECTIONISM

The recent global financial crisis could pose a serious threat to the trend of globalisation and free-trade. We may see an increase in protectionism.

Attitude shifts on free trade could potentially disrupt the world trade and economic system. Changing the way the world trades can have a major impact on global collaboration in research and development initiatives.

CONFLICTS IN AFGHANISTAN VERSUS STABILITY IN SWITZERLAND

Comparing Afghanistan and Switzerland is a novel demonstration of how conflict can be a spoiler for innovations that can help nations to develop and prosper. The longstanding perpetual conflict in Afghanistan continues to cripple the country's socio-economic development and progress. Today, Afghanistan is one of the poorest and least developed countries in the world, with a nominal GDP per capita of $428. Switzerland's stability has made it one of the richest countries in the world, with a nominal GDP per capita of $67,384. Switzerland is well-known for its high standard of living.

Table 4.1 shows the crippling effects of conflict on a country.

Both nations are landlocked and endowed with natural beauty. Switzerland is a landlocked alpine country with an area

Table 4.1:   Crippling effects of conflict.

Country	Political Situation	Size (sq km)	Population (millions)	Countries that shared borders	Per capita GDP	Total GDP Mi US$
Afghanistan	ongoing internal and external conflict	647,500	28.15	Iran Pakistan Turkmenistan Uzbekistan Tajikistan China	$428	12,048
Switzerland	no war since 1815	41,285	7.78	Germany France Italy Austria Liechtenstein	$67,384	524,443

of 41,285 square kilometres, surrounded by Germany to the north, Austria and Liechtenstein to the east, Italy to the south and France to the west. Since 1815, Switzerland has not been involved in any war.

Afghanistan is also a landlocked country surrounded by Turkmenistan, Uzbekistan and Tajikistan in the north, China in the far northeast, Pakistan in the east and south, and Iran in the south and west. It has an area of 647,500 square kilometres and a population of 28.15 million. Afghanistan has a rich history that began in 330 B.C. In 1919, Afghanistan declared independence. Since then, there has been a series of internal and external conflicts.

NON-MILITARY CONFLICT — CYBER CONFLICT

Conflicts will continue to evolve. Potential combatants have broader access to advances in science and technology due to improvements in information and communication technologies.

The increasing preference towards non-military means of conflict will likely result in cyber warfare.

Cyber-security issues and network science are and will be a new challenging area for research and development.

WATER SCARCITY AS A SOURCE OF CONFLICT

Several major rivers flow through multiple countries as they flow from their mountain sources to the sea. The sharing of rivers as a water source and for transportation is becoming more complex. Countries situated downstream are at the mercy of those situated upstream, since the usage habits of the latter determine the quality and volume of water that the former receives. Discord and disagreement on the sharing of rivers is a potential source of conflict between nations.

Water scarcity will be a source of conflict. With the current advances in desalination of sea water, rich countries would not run out of water. However, poorer countries would not be able to afford it. Researchers need to conduct research to discover cheaper and more cost-effective ways to bring down the price of water. Poor countries should not need to resort to war in order to secure adequate water supplies.

Water is a vital resource for human survival. As estimated by UN Water Statistics, one in every six people worldwide currently lacks safe drinking water. The demand for fresh water is set to rise as the world population grows in tandem with rapid industrialisation, urbanisation and climate changes. Decision-makers will have to give their unwavering attention to this growing water challenge.

CLIMATE CHANGE INDUCED CRISIS

A new spoiler in the form of climate change-induced crises such as the effects of rising sea levels, violent storms, droughts, floods, crop failures and mass migration can initiate events that lead to cross-border conflicts.

Over the next two to three decades, several regions have been identified as having high chances of being affected by climate change-induced crises. Major flooding of Bangladesh's river delta area can cause major damage to housing and infrastructure, lead to shortages of food and safe potable water, and cause the spread of contagious diseases. These climate change-induced crises could force hundreds of thousands of refugees to flee into neighbouring India. This mass exodus has the potential to ignite social unrest between Indian residents and Bangladeshi refugees, which in turn may escalate to border conflicts.

To mitigate climate change as a potential spoiler of innovation, there should be more research that emphasises the search for renewable energy sources as substitutes for fossil fuels to reduce greenhouse gas emissions. There have been negotiations that have focused on an international climate treaty, but there is no initiative or dialogue for security issues or potential conflicts that could arise as a result of climate change.

Security issues that arise from environmental and social impacts caused by global climate change are a potential spoiler in the 21st century.

CONFLICT AS A RESULT OF CONTROL OF ENERGY RESOURCES OR CURTAILING OF OIL/GAS SUPPLY

Countries have used their control of energy resources as weapons of coercion and political influence. A recent example was Russia's use of the gas pipeline network that links East Asia to Europe to exert and promote Russian interests and influence.

Nigeria's oil production is often disrupted by ethnic and political violence, as well as criminal activities.

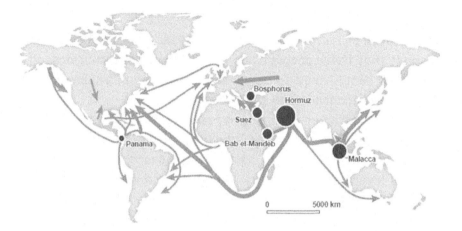

Figure 4.4:   The world's oil flows through six critical choke points.

The Suez Canal, the strait of Hormuz and the Straits of Malacca are vulnerable chokepoints in the oil export route that flows from the Middle East (see Figure 4.4).

The long logistical supply chain of pipeline, sea transportation of oil and gas are potential targets for pirates and terrorists.

The six choke points along the oil-transporting sea routes are:

1. Strait of Hormuz
2. Strait of Malacca
3. Bab el-Mandeb
4. Suez Canal and Sumed Pipeline
5. Bosphorus
6. Panama Canal

Given the world's major dependence on oil and gas, any disruption to smooth supplies of oil or gas will have a major impact on oil-importing countries.

Any escalation of conflicts or piracy that can cause disruptions in the flow of fuel supplies will have a major impact on social and economic developments, thereby causing delays in innovation initiatives.

Many of the conflicts in Asia originate from ethnic, religious, social or historical contexts. Lessons from history clearly suggest that these problems do not have absolute solutions, and that they simply need to be managed with the minimum amount of violence, economic and social costs.

One can consider investing in research that targets conflict management. To prevent the "spoilers" as far as possible from making any adverse impact, the global research community will need to leverage on education, research and innovation for the promotion of peace, international understanding, cooperation and security.

Chapter 5

THE WAY FORWARD

THE GLOBAL RESEARCH FOUNDATION

Asia is now the new global hub for innovation, setting trends and generating momentum. However, going forward in this direction will not be the most optimal solution in today's inter-connected world due to limited financial and human resources.

The optimal approach to creating knowledge and discovering new inventions to solve societal challenges depends on speed of access to the global pool of knowledge, networks of talent and available resources.

Nations are now developing or have developed respective science and technology (S&T) plans, each unique in the priori-ties that have been set in terms of funding and implementation. Many nations have begun setting targets for and measuring their R&D spending as a percentage of GDP in an effort to drive economic growth.

Moving forward towards a global community for innovation is desirable, since this will facilitate researchers of more than one nation in cooperation and collaboration on issues of common societal concern.

For funding, one model will be for each nation to contribute a fixed percentage of its GDP for the Global Research Foundation (GRF). In addition, philanthropists from around the world will be encouraged to contribute towards research in areas that they are passionate about and where they would want to make a significant contribution towards alleviating societal challenges.

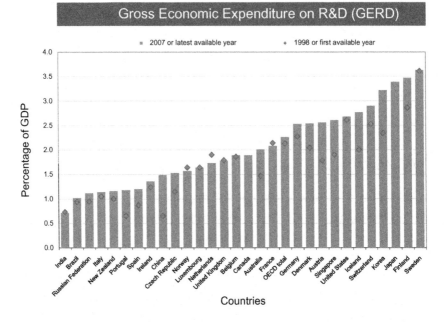

Figure 5.1: Gross economic expenditure on R&D (GERD).

Sources: OECD Factbook 2009: Economic, Environmental and Social Statistic: A*STAR Singapore.

With reference to Figure 5.1, we suggest that all countries agree to an acceptable percentage point of GERD, which should be at least 0.5%, to be dedicated to the GRF. This will focus on solving the most pressing key global challenges such as food, water, energy, healthcare, infectious diseases, information security and climate change (see Figure 5.2).

This model of global cooperation is the ideal method for finding solutions to address global challenges that have been brought about by the confluences of rapid population growth, urbanisation, limited water resources, energy and food shortages, healthcare and the advent of cyber communication.

What will bring nations together to work on common societal challenges in the globalised world of today?

Figure 5.2: Global societal challenges of the 21st century.

The generation of new knowledge and innovations for the common good of mankind that will create a better quality of life on planet Earth may be the "glue" that will bind mankind together.

The challenge lies in establishing strategic facilitation systems and processes that will act as enablers. We suggest the establishment of a GRF with the overarching goal of enabling researchers across the world to cooperate and compete to generate new knowledge and solutions to global challenges.

The world spends about US$ 1 trillion annually (about 1.6 percent of world GDP) on research and innovation. About 15 percent (about US$ 150 billion) of this is appropriated by various national governments for pre-competitive research in the public sector. Looking at the areas in which public sector research funds are expended in various countries, it is very clear that research funds are increasingly being allocated to areas such as healthcare, food, water, energy, urbanisation, cyber security, environment and climate change (see Figure 5.2). These priorities are similar or identical across most nations. This leads to the duplication of research efforts and inefficient use of precious research funds. Paradoxically, more research funds are needed in order to address complex global challenges. It makes sense for scientists to work together across the current boundaries that have been set by institutes and national funding agencies. Moreover, exchanges between scientists promote stronger and more positive ties between nations. The time is ripe for the establishment of a Global Research Fund to support international teams of researchers in conducting pre-competitive research. It is recommended that a collective pool of ten billion dollars should be set aside annually to support the start of a GRF. It is both timely and beneficial to have a global organisation manage this fund; as this will promote mutual trust between nations. Based on the experiences of various large-scale joint ventures of this nature, critics will say that this altruistic idea will not work and that it is unsustainable. Such views are legitimate and understandable.

Since World War II, the world has witnessed relative peace and stability, partly owing to the formation of several global organisations (see Figure 5.3). However inefficient and bureaucratic they may be, there is no doubt that they provide avenues for the resolution of international issues. The GRF's role as such an organisation will be to work towards finding solutions to global societal challenges through the use of research and innovation.

We also recommend the establishment of a Global Innovation Award (similar to the Nobel Prize in stature) that will be managed by the GRF. This will be a special world-class recognition award for global teams of researchers from more than two nations who work together to address global challenges in an impactful way.

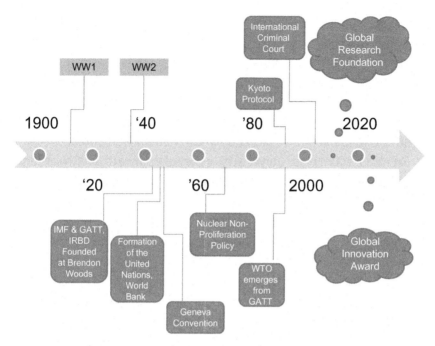

Figure 5.3: Global cooperation is the way forward — the Global Research Foundation and Global Innovation Award.

The discovery of new knowledge is a platform for win-win cooperation. The old concept of research being a zero-sum game has been rendered obsolete.

A prosperous world is a better world for everyone.

BOLD APPROACHES TOWARDS INTELLECTUAL PROPERTY

Out of the US$ 1 trillion spent on global research and development, it is reasonable to assume that about two-thirds is spent by the private sector and one-third is contributed by the public sector. Assuming that half the public sector spending — i.e. approximately over 150 billion dollars, approximately equivalent to about 0.25 percent of global GDP — is spent on pre-competitive research, which is mainly pursued in universities and institutions of higher learning around the world, we need a bold approach to manage new knowledge and discoveries.

University researchers report their research findings in peer-reviewed open literature which is accessible to others around the world. Their intellectual properties (IPs) are protected by patents and copyrights issued by their home institutions.

In most countries, university-generated inventions that have been funded by taxpayers are owned by the universities which employ the inventors. Over the years, many universities around the world, beginning with American universities, have set up technology licensing offices (TLOs). These TLOs are managed solely by respective universities or operated at arm's length as companies together with private sector participation. Typically, universities' TLOs own the patents and reserve the rights to make decisions to commercialise inventions. As more and more taxpayers' dollars are spent on public sector R&D, there is increasing pressure for university research to show tangible results. In order to gain a competitive edge over other nations, there is a growing expectation on university-generated research IPs to support local economic growth, create employment and solve societal challenges and needs. Naturally, these are pre-dictable expectations whenever public funds are involved.

Several universities' TLOs have set up IP policies and guidelines which spell out revenue sharing models to promote entrepreneurial spirit. Some TLOs have revenue sharing mod-els based on the sharing of net income. Some models have revenue sharing ratio of 50 percent to 75 percent for the inventor with the rest going to the institution. The net income is defined as gross income less indirect costs and all associated legal costs incurred during the filing of patents and the marketing costs of licensing.

On average, only less than 2 percent of university-generated IPs worldwide are exploited commercially. There are several reasons for this: ideas are ahead of their time, poor understanding of market opportunities and needs, the lack of funding support to develop an invention into a product, the lack of requisite management skills, over-protective nature of inventors, restrictive and time-consuming IP licensing practices in universities, the lack of commitment to follow through, the lack of an industrial base to leverage on university innovations, the lack of entrepreneurial talent and venture capital fund system, and so on. While these are legitimate justifications for the poor performance of university-generated IPs, we suggest fine-tuning current IP management practices worldwide.

Based on historical observations, it takes between 14 and 44 years to translate a new medical finding into clinical application. From a study between 1979 and 1983, only 5 percent of promising new discoveries actually become licensed for clinical use.[62] Overall, the median translation lag was about 24 years.

For engineering science, this average lag time worked out to be 15 years. From society's point of view, improvements have to be made to reduce this wasteful lag time.

In order to allow university-generated IPs flow to the market and society more effectively, we suggest the following mindset change in managing IPs:

1. Recognise that the inventor knows the invention or discovery best.
2. The inventor should take greater responsibility for IP protection by contributing part of the IP protection costs.
3. By default, the inventor owns the IP, not the university or institution of higher learning where he or she is employed. The inventor should take a proactive role in transferring IP to the private sector and/or exploit IP for commercial purposes.

---

[60] "Life Cycle of Translational Research Medical Interventions", 5 September 2008, Vol. 321, SCIENCE, published by AAAS.

4. The inventor should be given appropriate support to make right decisions in protecting and exploiting IP; the final decision on how the IP is to be exploited must rest on the inventor and not on third persons, who are unable to have a deep understanding of the invention and who do not have access to suitable industries and markets.

5. Nations and universities should adopt proactive and forward-looking policies to facilitate inventors in test-bedding their IPs while leveraging on benefits from the successful exploitation of IPs.

Our proposed approach is based on the principle that the inventor should be responsible when it comes to IP management. Our proposed approach forces inventors to appreciate market needs and global challenges more deeply and accurately, and thus enables them to fine-tune or re-prioritise research along the way, as most university researchers have an active research life of over 30 to 40 years.

Critics to this approach may say that this will lead to an over-emphasis on the commercialisation of research. University researchers will also be pressured to do more applied research than basic research and will be spending more of their time on non-research activities rather than low-quality research.

The principles on which public funding of university research is based can be used to address the concerns listed above. There should and will be ample room for university academics to pursue research for the pure advancement of knowledge. However, those university academics who are interested in protecting their IPs must be subjected to the IP management principles and expectations mentioned earlier in this chapter.

Epilogue

Looking back at history, it is abundantly clear that both ideas and innovations have enabled humans to progress over time. The world now spends about 1.5 percent of GDP on research and innovation, an amount that has surpassed US$ 1 trillion for the first time in human history. Worldwide, about 30 nations are actively spending 2 to 3 percent of national GDP on research and development. To secure their long-term well-being, many more nations need to commit to increased budgets to promote research and innovation. These budgets are considered smaller when compared to what nations spend on defence and healthcare. Nations should consider setting aside 5 percent of GDP for research and development, as this has a multitude of benefits in the form of long-term social advancement and the yielding of sustainable and novel solutions to societal challenges.

Like the developed nations, emerging Asian nations are also investing public funds in research and innovation in a bid to secure or maintain their competitive advantage and sustain economic growth. Since their resources mainly come from tax-payers, policy makers find it increasingly reasonable to direct resources to areas of research that address issues of national importance, such as job creation and economic growth. There will definitely be opposing voices to this approach. Some critics believe that research cannot be directed, nor can innovation be planned. They argue that scholarly pursuits are at their best when provided with independent financial support that is dedicated to producing immense benefits for society in the form of deeper knowledge. Apart from these few specific areas, all Asian nations face similar societal challenges at a broader level. The stakes that come with these challenges are high enough to attract brilliant minds from both the ranks of established scientists as well as the growing pool of talented young people — an essential partnership for research breakthroughs and innovation. Interestingly, the same set of influences is increasingly shaping the decisions of policy makers in the USA and Europe when it comes to allocating their national resources towards research and innovation. Given that both Asian and Western nations are faced with similar sets of influences, there are likely to be significant synergies in collaborative pre-competitive efforts between Asia and the rest of the world in addressing both domestic and international problems. The research community needs to be fully aware of societal challenges, and must engage in dialogues with all stakeholders to ensure that innovations are relevant to policies and societal needs.

A number of American universities are cradles of research excellence and innovation. Science and technology parks in the vicinity of universities contribute to both job creation and economic growth. Following the footsteps of America, more nations, especially Asian countries, are turning to universities to develop solutions to the aforementioned challenges that are facing us today. Until now, the majority of research in universities has been pursued within the narrow limits of traditional disciplines. It is becoming increasingly clear that solutions to societal challenges require active collaboration among different disciplines — physical sciences, biological sciences, medical sciences, engineering and technology, and humanities and social sciences. Universities must lead by example by encouraging scientific and non-scientific researchers to collaborate to address today's multi-faceted and multi-dimensional societal challenges.

Currently, most national governments spend only about 0.1 to 0.5 percent of GDP on research conducted at the universities or institutes of higher learning (IHLs). It is reasonable to conclude that the full potential of universities, in the form of their multi-disciplinary nature and access to talented, innovative young people, is not being tapped upon to generate new knowledge that can help to address global challenges. A higher proportion of national R&D spending should go towards research in IHLs. Universities are cradles of young minds, who will benefit immensely by working on global challenges, and who will in turn contribute to the nation's progress after their graduation. University-generated research results are reported in open and peer-reviewed scientific literature. Moreover, university-generated intellectual properties are also protected by patents and copyrights, thus allowing both firms and individuals to freely tap on these ideas and improve them so long as copyrights are not infringed.

Women are proportionally under-represented in the global research and innovation sector. Active efforts must be made to increase the number of women working in the research and innovation sector. This will have benefits beyond pure research and innovation, as better exposed and knowledgeable women will influence future generations to be more interested in learning, research and innovation, thus contributing to overall social advancement.

Earth's resources will come under increasing pressure as the size and expectations of the population continues to grow. Researchers and innovators are well-placed to identify ways and means to lower costs and utilise resources more efficiently. This would alleviate potential conflicts and facilitate equity to help mankind to continue prospering.

Asia has had a history of innovation, and the immense, readily available pool of research talent is poised to lead innovation into the third millennium.

Is this necessarily a good thing?

The world needs to come up with solutions to ensure a continued supply of basic necessities such as food, water and energy to a growing population. These solutions must also be sustainable in providing an environment that is conducive for urban living without degrading natural ecosystems.

As we continue our journey into the next millennium, we need to work towards a global innovation community.

We are now faced with major global challenges (see Figure E.1).

What will the future be like if there were a paradigm shift from regional to global innovation?

Imagine a global repository of knowledge, with the best minds in universities, the private and public sectors working together in a multi-disciplinary context to focus on finding solutions that meet the needs of society.

Figure E.1: Major global challenges.

The 21st century will be full of new discoveries of sustainable solutions for the global population, all in the spirit of innovation and adventure.

We should work towards adopting a borderless, visionary approach towards finding novel solutions to societal challenges.

The global economic created a new environment and demonstrated the intimate connectedness and interdependency of all regions.

A paradigm shift in mindset is required for us to shift our focus from a national to a global agenda, one that seeks to solve global challenges through innovations. It is certainly desirable for more people to be connected globally in order to launch innovations that are of lasting value to mankind. International networking and interaction between leading minds will help establish a more efficient model for collaboration on beneficial research.

The thrust and focus of public policy makers on education, science and innovation for the common good will go a long way towards preparing all for a brighter future.

Worldwide innovation is not a zero-sum game; we all benefit by building on each others' good ideas and leveraging on each others' talent and passion to contribute towards the greater good of mankind.

BIBLIOGRAPHY

21st Century Technologies : Promises and Perils of a Dynamic Future. (1998). Paris: Organisation for Economic Co-operation and Development.

2009 Global R&D Funding Forecast (2008). R&D Magazine.

Adams, J., King, C. & Ma, N. (2009). *Global Research Report: China.* Leeds, UK: Thomson Reuters.

Bunch, B. H. (1993). *The Timetables of Technology : A Chronology of the Most Important People and Events in the History of Technology* (Vol. 819399). New York: Simon & Schuster.

Chinese Academy of Social Sciences. (2009). *The Blue Book of Cities in China — Annual Report of Urban Development of China.* Beijing, China: Chinese Academy of Social Sciences.

Contopoulos-Ioannidis, D. G., Alexiou, G. A., Gouvias, T. C., & Ioannidis, J. P. A. (2008). Medicine — Life cycle of translational research for medical interventions. *Science, 321*(5894), 1298–1299.

A Decade of Reform : Science and Technology Policy in China. (1997). Ottawa, Ont.: International Development Research Centre.

Dehoff, K. & Jaruzelski, B. (2008). *Beyond Borders: The Global Innovation 1000.* New York: Booz & Company.

Drexler, K. E. (2007). *Technology and Society : Issues for the 21st Century and Beyond Engines of Creation* (3rd ed.). Upper Saddle River, N. J., Garden City, N. Y.: Prentice Hall.

Immelt, J. R., Govindarajan, V. & Timble, C. (2009). How GE is disrupting itself. *Harvard Business Review,* October 2009.

The Economic Impact & Social Benefits of University of California, Berkeley. (2005–2006). University of California, Berkeley.

Education and Inequality Across Europe. (2009). Cheltenham: Edward Elgar.

Education at a Glance : OECD Indicators. (2009). Paris: Organisation for Economic Co-operation and Development.

Gribbin, J. R. (2008). *The Britannica Guide to the 100 Most Influential Scientists*. London: Robinson/Running Press.

The Impact of the University of Cambridge on the UK Economy and Society. (2006). Cambridge: Library House, in Association with East of England Development Agency, University of Cambridge, Cambridge Network and Greater Cambridge Partnership.

League of European Research Universities. (2003). *Research Intensive Universities as Engines for the "Europe of Knowledge"*. Belgium: League of European Research Universities.

MacKay, D. J. C. (2007). *Taking Sides Sustainable Energy : Without the Hot Air* (4th ed.). Dubuque, IA; Cambridge, England: UIT Cambridge.

Maddison, A. (2001). *Sustainable Development : Critical Issues*. Paris: Organisation for Economic Co-operation and Development.

Melbourne Vice-Chancellors' Forum. (2007). *Melbourne — Australia's Knowledge Capital: The Contributions of Melbourne's Universities to the City's Economic, Cultural and Community Development*. Melbourne: Howard Partners Pty Ltd.

National Survey of R&D in Singapore 2007. (2008). Singapore: Agency for Science, Technology and Research.

National Survey of R&D Survey in Singapore 2008. (2009). Singapore: Agency for Science, Technology and Research.

Needham, J. (1978). *The Shorter Science and Civilisation in china : An Abridgement of Joseph Needham's Original Text* (Vol. 51813). Cambridge, New York: Cambridge University Press.

Organization for Economic Cooperation and Development. (2009). *OECD Factbook 2009: Economic, Environmental and Social Statistics*. Paris: OECD Publishing.

Perez, C. (2002). *Technological Revolutions and Financial Capital: The Dynamics of Bubbles and Golden Ages*. Northampton, MA: Edward Elgar.

Press Release Guide, Flash Memory Summit, Santa Clara, California: August 12–14. (2008). Santa Clara, California.

Resek, R., Hewings, G. J. D., Lubotsky, D., & Edwards, F. (2009). *The Impact of the University of Illinois on the Economy of Our State*. Urbana-Champaign: Institute of Government and Public Affairs, University of Illinois.

Schaeffer, R. K. (2009). *Understanding Globalization: The Social Consequences of Political, Economic, and Environmental Change* (4th ed.). Lanham, Md.: Rowman & Littlefield Publishers.

Schuller, T., & Desjardins, R. (2007). *Understanding the Social Outcomes of Learning*. Paris: OECD.

Science & Technology Plan 2010: Sustaining Innovation-Driven Growth. (2010). Singapore: Ministry of Trade and Industry.

Slaughter, S. (2004). *Academic Capitalism and the New Economy: Markets, State, and Higher Education*. Baltimore: Johns Hopkins University Press.

Slaughter, S., & Leslie, L. L. (1997). *Academic Capitalism : Politics, Policies, and the Entrepreneurial University*. Baltimore: Johns Hopkins University Press.

The State of Food Insecurity in the World 2009. (2009). Rome: Food and Agriculture Organization of the United Nations.

Tambyah, S. K. (2009). *The Wellbeing of Singaporeans : Values, Lifestyles, Satisfaction and Quality of Life*. New Jersey: World Scientific.

Technology & the Future. (2006). (10th ed.). Belmont, CA: Thomson/ Wadsworth.

Tertiary Education for the Knowledge Society: Synthesis Report. (2008). Paris: Organisation for Economic Co-operation and Development.

Vincent-Lancrin, S. (2006). What is Changing in Academic Research? Trends and Futures Scenarios. *European Journal of Education, 41*(2), 169–202.

WIPO Economic Studies Statistics and Analysis Division. (2009). *World Intellectual Property Indicators 2009*. Geneva, Switzerland: World Intellectual Property Organization.

World Bank, & International Finance Corporation. (2008). *Doing Business 2009 : Comparing Regulation in 181 Economies.* Washington, D.C.: World Bank Publications.

World Development Indicators. (1973). Washington, D.C.: International Bank for Reconstruction and Development.

WEB RESOURCES

Name	Web Resource
American Association for the Advancement of Science	http://www.aaas.org/
Asian Development Bank	http://www.adb.org/
Battelle	http://www.battelle.org/
Booz & Co.- Global Innovation 1000	http://www.booz.com/
China Ministry of Science and Technology	http://www.most.gov.cn/eng/
Chinese Academy of Sciences	http://english.cas.cn/
Doing Business, The World Bank and International Finance Corporation	http://www.doingbusiness.org/
European Research Council (ERC)	http://erc.europa.eu/
International Energy Agency (IEA)	http://www.iea.org/
ISI Web of Knowledge, Thomson Reuters	http://www.isiwebofknowledge.com/
Lien Foundation	http://www.lienfoundation.org/
National Institute of Health (NIH)	http://www.nih.gov/
National Research Foundation, Singapore	http://www.nrf.gov.sg/
National University of Singapore	http://www.nus.edu.sg/
New 7 Wonders	http://www.new7wonders.com/
Organization for Economic Co-operation and Development (OECD)	http://www.oecd.org/
Population Reference Bureau	http://www.prb.org/

Scopus	http://www.scopus.com/
Singapore - Public Utility Board (PUB)	http://www.pub.gov.sg/
Singapore Economic Development Board	http://www.edb.gov.sg/
Tata Motors - Nano	http://tatanano.inservices. tatamotors.com/tatamotors/
THE - QS World University Rankings	http://www.topuniversities.com/
Thomson Reuters	http://science.thomsonreuters.com/
UN Population Division	http://www.un.org/esa/population/
Water.org	http://water.org/
World Bank	http://www.worldbank.org/
World Gold Council	http://www.gold.org/
World Intellectual Property Organization	http://www.wipo.int
World Mapper	http://www.worldmapper.org/

Key Definitions

Innovation has been described as the creative use of various forms of knowledge when responding to market-articulated demands and other social needs (OECD 1999a).